MISSIONARIES IN THE MISSION OF GOD

by

E. Elbert Smith

A special thanks to my wife, Kay,
for continuing the journey of following Him
together to another continent,
and for sharing in the
preparation of this
material and
manuscript.

Missionaries in the Mission of God
Acts 1:1-2
Table of Contents

MISSIONARIES IN THE MISSION OF GOD

Their questions were understandable and obvious. As I had the opportunity to spend time over fifteen years with new workers on the way to the field, we would unpack the New Testament's picture of how the kingdom expanded, how churches were planted in the book of Acts. But what about ministering to the poor? What about intentionally ministering to the suffering, those caught in human trafficking, fighting for social justice or climate issues? How does that fit into the missionary task? Over and over, I found it necessary to give short answers that put these details in place biblically. Then, one of the first assignments after moving to England to train was to develop the topic more fully.[1] When I took the time to carefully unpack the mission of God and how missionaries, and the missionary task, fit in a balanced way into that mission, the response of the new colleagues was very encouraging. I am putting down in detail the content from that meeting.

Scripture is an amazing treasure because it gives us God's thoughts, God's perspective, God's word in black and white. We are extremely blessed to have times when the presence of the Holy Spirit is palpable, and it seems as if we nearly hear a literal voice. Isaiah spoke of hearing a voice behind us saying, this is the way, walk in it (Isa 30:21). As believers we often desire to know God's will so clearly and rejoice when that is our experience. However, anytime God's guidance is filtered through me, through subjective experience, fallible humanity, I am extremely aware that an element of uncertainty has been inserted. I know God is infallible but am extremely aware I am not. Not so with Scripture. With Scripture we have "the Word of God!" No wonder believers have affirmed that the norm for faith and practice, both what we believe and what we do, is the Word of God!

There is no area of life where human beings do not need God's perspective, understanding or guidance. However, in the area of missions we are certainly in need. There are a host of good opinions from very well-meaning people. We are uncomfortable thinking anyone's view is not right. But it is so very comforting to remember that we are not left to sort through this topic with our own wisdom, any more than we are left to decide what truth is about any other topic. God's word is the perfect treasure to help us think clearly about faith and practice, what to think and what to do, in the area of missions.

The four Gospels provide the inspired details of Jesus' earthly life. While some details of the following years are included in the Epistles, it is the book of Acts that provides "the second volume of a *History of Christian Origins.*"[2] While Matthew, Mark and John provide details of Jesus' life, Luke-Acts provides that *and* the history of the next thirty years: the expansion of the church from Jerusalem all the way around to Rome. In the first verse of Acts, Luke the Physician (Col 4:14; 2 Tim 4:11) refers to "all that Jesus began to do and teach" and then in the following verse he mentions "the apostles whom he had chosen." By exploring the first phrase we will find a description of all the things that Jesus did and taught. In so doing we will discuss the extensive mission of God and how believers can fit into God's mission. By exploring the second phrase, we will consider how Acts describes the twelve apostles but, also, specifically describes others as apostles, sent-out ones or missionaries. In this exploration we will discover the New Testament's teaching about missionaries as part of the mission of God.

"ALL THAT JESUS BEGAN TO DO AND TEACH" ACTS 1:1

As believers, we know that God is causing all things to work together for good, specifically so that we will be "conformed to the image of his Son" (Rom 8:29). Since we know that God is working in this way in our lives, we want to lean into what God is doing and not to resist him in his work. Since we are being made to be more like Jesus, it helps us to know him better and better, to be soft clay as God conforms us to his image. It proves helpful for us to regularly go to the gospels to think about him, to worship him, to consider him (Heb 12:3).

In the opening phrase of Acts, Luke reminds of what he included in the first volume, the Gospel According to Luke. He describes there "all that Jesus began to do and teach." The wording is beautiful. Jesus has not stopped doing and teaching. The end of the gospel was not the end of Jesus' doing and teaching. He continued doing and teaching through Acts. We are now the body of Christ (Col 1:18). He lives the Christ-life through us (Gal 2:20). As we reflect on what the Gospels, and Luke in particular, tell us that Jesus began to do and teach, we will be reminded of some of what he continues to do and teach today.[3] This seems consistent with the Old Testament concept that we should study God's works or all the mission of God.[4] However, we will want to be sure and remember Jesus' interpretation of God's working that He provided at the end of Luke's gospel.[5]

As we think about the works of God it helps us to remember that the Holy Spirit has gifted every believer to be enabled spiritually to participate in what God is doing. Now, unique gifting always needs to be thought about in a manner consistent with God's commands. God also provides opportunities or assignments in which we find ourselves in life.[6] These all fit together to help believers understand how they can best fit into the works or the mission of God.

CHAPTER ONE: WHAT DID JESUS DO AND TEACH?

As Luke began the book of Acts, he dropped a short phrase that provides his insight (inspired by the Spirit) into what was contained in the Gospel According to Luke. "In my former book, Theophilus, I wrote about *all that Jesus began to do and to teach*" (Acts 1:1). A walk through the gospel will remind us of the things that Jesus did and taught during His three-year ministry. Thinking about all that Jesus did, as God-incarnate, reminds us that the Old Testament encourages us to study the works of God. While these broad topics lead in many different directions, Jesus Himself made clear that they are not as random as some might think. Instead, they have a purpose, or a focus, that Jesus explicitly provides.

Luke, like an excellent teacher, provides a spot for the reader to remember what was in the first volume before he launches into the second. The connection helps us see the flow from Jesus' life to the early church. The connection helps us to see what God is up to today, because the gospel recorded what He *began to do and to teach*. As John Polhill points out, "The work and words of Jesus continue throughout Acts in the ministry of the apostles and other faithful Christian witnesses. It still goes on in the work of the church today."[7] I like to ask people at this point to list their favorite things that Jesus did while he walked on earth. Quite often, we remember the broad categories that an outline reveals. Jesus fed the five thousand. He cast out demons and healed the sick. Jesus raised the dead! He showed tender compassion to the hurting. He confronted religious hypocrisy. He walked steadfastly to the cross and triumphed over death on the third day! He appeared to his disciples and gave them marching orders.

However, better than a random list of what Jesus did, let's take time to review what Luke recorded that Jesus did and taught.

The first three chapters of Luke's gospel set the stage for "all that Jesus began to do and teach." Luke provides the most detailed description of Jesus' birth and the only description of his childhood. He carefully begins declaring Jesus' place in history[8] and his identity as God the Son.[9] Chapter two ends with the twelve-year-old Jesus declaring that he had to be about his Father's business. In Luke three, John the Baptist cries in the wilderness, "Prepare the way of the Lord," and says that the one coming after him will "baptize you with the Holy Spirit and fire." After John baptizes Jesus, the voice of God the Father declares to Jesus, "You are my beloved Son; with you I am well pleased." Luke then solidifies Jesus' place in history with his genealogical ties to David, Abraham, and Adam.

In Luke four, Jesus begins his ministry by victoriously facing temptation in the wilderness. The text puts an emphasis on the Holy Spirit that prepares us for the way the book of Acts will continue that same emphasis. "And Jesus *full of the Holy Spirit*, returned from the Jordan and was *led by the Spirit* in the wilderness" (Luke 4:1). Jesus responded victoriously to temptation with Scripture, by saying each time, "it is written."

In the next scene of chapter four, Jesus began his Galilean ministry[10] being rejected in the synagogue at Nazareth. Basing his identity on Scripture, Jesus said, "The Spirit of the Lord is upon me, because he has anointed me to proclaim good news to the poor. He has sent me to proclaim liberty to the captives and recovering of sight to the blind, to set at liberty those who are oppressed, to proclaim the year of the Lord's favor" (Luke 4:18-19; Isa 61:1-2). Jesus returned to this same Isaiah passage three chapters later in Luke's gospel when the disciples of John the Baptist ask about Jesus' identity. "Go and tell John what you have seen and heard: the blind receive their sight, the lame walk, lepers are cleansed, and the deaf

8

hear, the dead are raised up, the poor have good news preached to them" (Luke 7:22). Jesus described the preaching of the gospel combined with compassionate ministry to suffering people (ministry that was miraculous and identified who Jesus was)! Jesus grounded his identity by pointing to Scripture, then pointed back to the same Scripture and clarified that he had been doing what Scripture said. However, the specific reason Jesus was rejected at Nazareth was not for making the connection to Isaiah sixty-one, but because he pointed out God's love for other ethnicities, even in the Old Testament. Elijah helped a widow of Sidon (Luke 4:25-26), and Elisha healed a leper from Syria (Luke 4:27-30). Jesus casts out the unclean spirit, who identified him as "the Holy One of God," from a man in Capernaum and then heals Peter's mother-in-law (Luke 4:31-39). As chapter four ends, many sick were brought to him and Jesus "laid his hands on every one of them and healed them" (Luke 4:40). He cast out demons (Luke 4:41) then refused the crowds' pleas to stay, saying, "I must preach the good news of the kingdom of God to other towns as well; for I was sent for this purpose" (Luke 4:43). *The first chapter describing what Jesus began to do and teach describes Jesus' modeling how to be victorious over sin, teaching in a way that stretched the religious to move beyond their comfort zones, ministering to the needs of the sick and oppressed, while maintaining his focus on being sent to other places and people.*

Chapters five through seven continue to clarify Jesus' identity, to fill in the details of Jesus' response to John's disciples. Following a miraculous catch of fish, Jesus promises Peter and Andrew, James and John, they will fish for men, calling them to be his disciples (Luke 5:1-11), and later calling Levi or Matthew (Luke 5:27-32). Jesus cleansed a leper and modeled withdrawing to pray (Luke 5:12-16). He healed a paralytic, after first forgiving his sins (Luke 5:17-26). While many descriptions of miracles do not specify motives, Jesus healed this man "so that"[11] those present would know that he had the right to do what only God could do: forgive sins.[12] After attending the feast at Levi's house, Jesus continued to stretch the Jewish leaders to put new wine "into fresh wineskins" (Luke 5:33-39). In Luke chapter six, Jesus was challenged by the Jewish leaders and clearly stated, "The Son of Man is lord of the Sabbath" (Luke 6:1-5). He healed a man with a withered, right hand on the Sabbath, filling the religious leaders with fury (Luke 6:6-11). He then spent the night in prayer and named the twelve apostles (Luke 6:12-16). Again, many sick were brought to him and he "healed them all" (Luke 6:17-19). Afterward he preached the good news to the poor, teaching his disciples how to live in the kingdom, in the sermon on the plain. Love your enemies. Bless those who curse you. Pray for those who abuse you. Turn the other cheek. Give to those who ask. Do to others as you wish to be done by. Judge not lest you be judged. Give and it will be given to you (Luke 6:20-49). As chapter seven begins, Jesus heals a Roman, Gentile, centurion's servant (Luke 7:1-10), before having compassion on a widow and raising her son from the dead, in the middle of his funeral procession (Luke 7:11-17)! Then the messengers come from John the Baptist with his question about Jesus' identity. "In that hour [Jesus] healed many people of diseases and plagues and evil spirits, and on many who were blind he bestowed sight. And he answered them, 'Go and tell John what you have seen and heard: the blind receive their sight, the lame walk, lepers are cleansed, and the deaf hear, the dead are raised up, the poor have good news preached to them'" (Luke 7:18-23). The chapter ends with Jesus' defense of John's ministry (Luke 7:24-35) and his forgiving an immoral woman's sins (Luke 7:36-50).

Chapters eight and nine end the first half of Luke's gospel and begin the journey to Jerusalem, for the cross, resurrection, and his return to heaven. Luke, having previously emphasized Jesus' compassion for, and ministry to, the poor and the foreigner, begins chapter eight specifically stating the prominent role of women in Jesus' ministry (Luke 8:1-3). Next, he continues to teach about kingdom multiplication and life in the kingdom with the parable of the sower and other parables (8:4-18). Jesus' mother comes and provides him an opportunity to put her in a special place of honor, but he does the opposite: "But he answered them, 'My mother and my brothers are those who hear the word of God and do it'" (Luke 8:20). Luke emphatically portrays Jesus as Lord over nature (with the calming of the sea, Luke 8:22-25), Lord over demons (with the healing of the Gadarene demoniac, sending him home to tell, Luke 8:26-39), Lord over disease (with the healing of the woman with the twelve-year discharge of blood, Luke 8:40-48) and Lord over death (with the raising of Jairus' twelve-year-old daughter from the dead, Luke 8:49-56).[13] Luke continues to describe Jesus making disciples as he sends out the twelve apostles to preach and heal, their beginning to put into practice that which he had been modeling for them (Luke 9:1-10). After a day of teaching and healing, Jesus feeds the five thousand (Luke 9:10-17) and was praying alone when Peter confesses that Jesus is the Christ of God (Luke 9:18-20). Jesus began to teach unambiguously that he was going to be crucified and raised the third day (Luke 9:21-22) and that following him requires his disciples to take up their crosses daily (Luke 9:23-27). Then Jesus went up on a mountain to pray with Peter, James, and John. His face was transfigured and began to shine like the sun (Matt 17:2). Moses and Elijah appeared and spoke of Jesus' departure for heaven. Peter, James, and John saw Jesus' glory and heard God the Father identify him, "This is my Son, my Chosen One; listen to him!" (Luke 9:28-36). Coming down from the mountain, Jesus heals a boy with an unclean spirit (Luke 9:37-43), repeats the teaching about his death (Luke 9:44-45), then settles an argument and misunderstanding among the disciples (Luke 9:46-50). Luke concludes the first portion of his gospel focused on Jesus' identity. With 9:51, Luke begins the second half of the gospel, Jesus' journey to Jerusalem, to the cross, the resurrection, and ascension. "When the days drew near for him to be taken up, he set his face to go to Jerusalem" (Luke 9:51).

What does the first segment of Luke's gospel describe about what Jesus began to do and teach? He taught about the kingdom and how to live life abundantly and victoriously. He met physical needs: fed the hungry, healed the sick, cast out demons; and made disciples, modeling how to live life. However, he did all the above with a clarity of being sent for a purpose. He did all the above clarifying who he was and repeatedly teaching that he came to die and rise again.

Luke begins the second part of his gospel describing Jesus sending out the unnamed seventy-two with the assurance that the "harvest is plentiful" (Luke 10:2), knowing they were going "as lambs in the midst of wolves" (Luke 10:3) to preach and heal, looking for a person of peace (Luke 10:6). In response to a religious expert, Jesus affirms that love for the Lord and one's neighbor summarizes the law (Luke 10:25-28) and tells the parable of the Good Samaritan to identify one's neighbor. (Luke 10:29-37). The chapter ends with the incident of Martha's distraction with much serving and Mary's choosing the main thing of being with Jesus and listening to his teaching (Luke 10:38-42). Jesus continued to model prayer, so much so that his disciples asked him to ***teach*** them to pray (Luke 11:1-13). After Jesus cast out a demon that was mute, some in the crowds falsely accused him and he announced that because he was casting out demons by the power of God "then the kingdom of God has come upon you" (Luke 11:14-26). Again, Jesus refused to agree when someone praised his mother (Luke 11:27-28). Jesus condemned a generation seeking for a sign, saying "no sign will be given to it except the sign of Jonah" (Luke 11:29-32). Jesus ***taught*** his disciples about receiving the light and pronounced woes on the Pharisees (Luke 11:33-54). He ***warned*** about hypocrisy (Luke 12:1-3) and ***taught*** his disciples not to fear men because the Holy Spirit will "teach you in that very hour" of persecution (Luke 12:4-12). Jesus refused to get involved in an inheritance dispute and *taught* with the parable of the rich fool and the need not to be anxious, but "instead, seek his kingdom and these things will be added to you" (Luke 12:13-34). Jesus *taught* his disciples to be ready for the Lord's coming, reminding them again he causes division (Luke 12:35-59). Jesus continued teaching in Judea, in chapter thirteen, saying, "unless you repent, you will all likewise perish," followed by the parable of the barren fig tree (Luke 13:1-9). While *teaching* on the Sabbath, Jesus *healed* a woman who had been bent over for eighteen years due to an evil spirit. He continued *teaching* about the kingdom with the parables of the mustard seed and leaven (Luke 13:10-21).

Jesus continued his journey to Jerusalem (Luke 13:22) emphasizing the need to enter by the narrow door (Luke 13:23-30). When told Herod wanted to kill him, Jesus was undeterred and lamented over Jerusalem's unwillingness to receive him (Luke 13:31-35). One Sabbath Jesus healed a man in a Pharisee's home. He then taught about humility, with the parable of the guests at a wedding feast, and the need to accept God's invitation, with the parable of guests who excused themselves (Luke 14:1-24). Jesus taught the large crowds traveling with him about the cost of being a disciple: "Whoever does not bear his own cross and come after me cannot be my disciple" (Luke 14:25-35). In response to the sinners drawing near to Jesus, the Pharisees grumbled. Jesus used the occasion to teach about God's love for the lost with the parables of the lost sheep, lost coin, and the prodigal son. He taught his disciples with the parable of the shrewd manager, concluding "no servant can serve two masters, for either he will hate the one and love the other, or he will be devoted to the one and despise the other. You cannot serve God and money" (Luke 16:1-13). The Pharisees, who loved money, ridiculed him. Jesus clarified "the Law and the Prophets were until John" and repeated his teaching about divorce, before teaching about eternal abodes with the Rich Man and Lazarus (Luke

16:14-30). Jesus taught his disciples about forgiveness, and they asked him to increase their faith (Luke 17:1-10).

Continuing on the way to Jerusalem (Luke 17:11), Jesus healed ten lepers and visited with the one, foreigner, who returned to thank him (Luke 17:12-19). Jesus then continued teaching the disciples about his second coming (Luke 17:22-37). Jesus again taught his disciples to pray, with the parable of the persistent widow and the tax collector who went home justified (Luke 18:1-14). Jesus permitted children to be brought to him but allowed the rich, young, ruler to depart (Luke 18:15-30). For the third time, Jesus foretold his death and third-day resurrection (Luke 18:31-34). At Jericho, blind Bartimaeus refused to be silenced and followed Jesus, after receiving his sight (Luke 18:35-43). While there, Zacchaeus, another hated tax collector, came to salvation, and Jesus said, "For the Son of Man came to seek and to save the lost" (Luke 19:1-10). "Because they supposed that the kingdom of God was to appear immediately," Jesus then told a parable about ten servants who received ten minas from their master who went to a distant country to receive for himself a kingdom. Upon his return, those who were faithful were rewarded but those who were not were condemned (Luke 19:11-27).

The journey to Jerusalem continues to shed light on "all that Jesus began to do and teach." While Luke continues to describe Jesus' miracles (five miracles in the ten chapters from ten to nineteen) there are far fewer miracles than previously (eighteen miracles recorded in the six chapters from four to nine). Similarly, while Luke recorded Jesus speaking in less than half of the verses in Luke 4-9 (45%), he records Jesus speaking in the majority of the verses in Luke 10-19 (80%). The Galilean ministry came to a crescendo declaring Jesus' identity with Peter's confession followed by the Transfiguration in chapter nine. However, the journey to Jerusalem focuses on what is ahead: death, burial, and ascension. These chapters are filled with teaching about the Good Samaritan identifying one's neighbor,

Mary listening at Jesus' feet was more important than a preoccupation with serving, clarifying that his casting out demons was proof that the kingdom of God had come, the dangers of religiosity, the normalcy of persecution, the need to be ready for his return and to look forward to that day. Jesus focused on teaching his disciples about bearing their cross, the Father's heart for the lost, the distraction of riches, and the clarity that comes from thinking about eternal realities. Yes, Luke records the healing of the ten lepers, but highlights that the only grateful one was a foreigner. Jesus welcomed the lowly children and sinful tax collector, but allowed the rich, young, ruler to walk away. And Jesus continued to teach about the second coming and the need to be faithful. "All that Jesus began to do and teach" in these chapters seemed to be less about doing and more about making disciples who were focused on eternity.

We are walking through the Gospel According to Luke with the focus of considering what Luke was pointing to when he began volume two of his history saying that in the first volume he had "dealt with all that Jesus began to do and teach" (Acts 1:1). The first three chapters of Luke dealt with his birth, childhood, and heritage. In chapter four he began to describe Jesus' ministry: the Galilean ministry (chapters four through nine) filled with miraculous meeting of peoples' needs; and then the journey to Jerusalem (chapters ten through nineteen) with some miracles but primarily teaching, making disciples, and preparing them to faithfully serve until Jesus' return. Then Luke, like the other gospel writers, spends a great deal of time on that one week, starting with the Sunday when Jesus' entered Jerusalem, ending one Sunday later, when the cross, grave, and resurrection were already finished!

Passion Week began with the triumphal entry when the multitude lined the road with palm branches and cried out, Hosanna (Luke 19:28-40)! As Jesus neared the city, he wept over it and described the destruction that was going to come forty years later (Luke 19:41-44). On the following day, Jesus cleansed the temple quoting Isaiah fifty-six, "'My house shall be a house of prayer,' but you have made it a den of robbers" (Isa 56:7; Luke 19:46). As Jesus taught in the temple he was challenged about his authority. He answered the question with a question about John's authority and then told the parable of the wicked tenants (Luke 20:1-18). The scribes asked him about paying taxes (Luke 20:19-26) and the Sadducees about the resurrection, and he asked about the Psalm where David called the Christ his Lord (Luke 20:27-44). Luke ends chapter twenty recounting Jesus' warning to beware of hypocritical religious teachers (Luke 20:45-47). After praising the widow's generous giving in the majestic temple (Luke 21:1-4), Jesus foretold the coming destruction of the temple and Jerusalem (Luke 21:5-24), his return, and the need to be watchful (Luke 21:25-38). In chapter twenty-two, Luke describes Judas' agreement to betray Jesus (Luke 22:1-6), the Passover and the Lord's Supper (Luke 22:7-23), Jesus settling the dispute over who was greatest, and foretelling Peter's denial (Luke 22:24-34). Jesus updated the instructions previously given regarding the person-of-peace (Luke 22:35-38), before going to the Mount of Olives to cry out to the Father in prayer (Luke 22:39-46). Judas, one of his twelve, led the soldiers who arrested Jesus (Luke 22:47-49). The last miracle that Jesus did, recorded in Luke's gospel,[14] the only one in this final section, was Jesus compassionately healing the ear of one who came to arrest him (Luke 22:50). Peter denied Jesus three times (Luke 22:54-62). Jesus was brought before the Sanhedrin (Luke 22:66-71), then Pilate, who declared him not guilty (Luke 23:1-5). After sending him to Herod, Pilate declared Jesus not guilty a second time (Luke 23:6-16). The chief priests and the mob continued to cry out for Jesus' death. Pilate declared him not guilty for the third time... and then gave into the multitude's cries turning Jesus over to be crucified (Luke 23:18-24).

Luke records Jesus telling the women following him to Golgotha not to weep for him, but for their children (Luke 23:26-31). With three words,

Luke described Jesus' being put on the cross: "they crucified him." Luke then recorded Jesus' first words from the cross: "Father, forgive them, for they know not what they do." Then comes the promise to the thief at his side, "today you will be with me in Paradise" (Luke 23:32-43). With three short verses, Luke records three hours of darkness, the curtain of the temple being torn in two, and Jesus' last words from the cross: "Father, into your hands I commit my spirit" (Luke 23:44-46). The supervising Roman centurion declared his innocence (Luke 23:44-49). Joseph of Arimathea asked for the body of Jesus, "wrapped it in a linen shroud and laid him in a tomb." The women from Galilee prepared spices and ointments, and rested on the Sabbath (Luke 23:50-56).

On the third day, the first day of the week, the women went into the tomb but "they did not find the body of Jesus." Two angels explained to them, "He is not here, but has risen," and reminded them of his repeated promises. Peter (and John) ran to the tomb and also saw it was empty (Luke 24:1-12; John 20:3-10). Later that day, as Cleopas and an unnamed disciple were walking on the road to Emmaus, Jesus began walking with them. They described the weekend's events concerning "Jesus the Nazarene, a man who was a prophet mighty in *work* and word."[15] Jesus then walked them through all the Old Testament passages concerning himself. Immediately after he vanished from their sight, they returned to Jerusalem telling the eleven and the group with them that they had seen the risen Lord (Luke 24:13-35). As they were speaking, Jesus himself appeared in their midst, inviting them to look at his hands and feet, to touch him, and then he ate a piece of fish before their eyes. He reminded them that he had repeatedly told them that "everything written about me in the Law of Moses and the Prophets and the Psalms must be fulfilled" (Luke 24:36-44).[16]

Luke bridges the gospel and the Acts of the Apostles explaining that he had specifically, intentionally recorded in the gospel "all that Jesus began to do and teach." We have walked through the chapters in the gospel describing Jesus' ministry with an eye to remembering what Luke, inspired by the Holy Spirit, included under that heading. If these are things that Jesus **began** to do and teach, the implication is clear that these are all things that Jesus is continuing to do and teach.[17] Since we as believers are members of his body and he is the head of the body, the things he did and taught could be something that he does through us, or others in his body, today. There is a breadth to all that Jesus began to do and teach. Obviously, he was carefully making disciples in the pages of Luke and is making disciples today. On the pages of Luke, he taught to love, forgive, give to the poor, and seek the kingdom of God. He is still teaching each of those things today through the body of Christ. Jesus was moved by compassion and acted to meet people's needs. Across the generations and globe, Jesus has moved his followers to see peoples' needs and to meet them. In John fourteen, the night before the cross, Jesus connected his works with our working in a beautiful promise: "Truly, truly, I say to you, whoever believes in me will also do the works that I do; and greater works than these will he do, because I am going to the Father" (John 14:12). While Jesus, God the Son, was limited to being in one place by his human body, believers are in every corner of the globe empowered by God the Spirit.

While Luke particularly pointed to the third gospel, as he began Acts, the same is true of what any of the gospels recorded about all that Jesus began to do and teach. Matthew's description of Jesus' conversation with the disciples of John begins, "Now when John, while imprisoned, heard of the works of Christ" (Matt 11:2, NASB).[18] John heard of the "works of Christ," and that is what we have just done. We have heard anew of the works of Christ. Matthew wrote his gospel to a Jewish audience, and he used a word that was found repeatedly in the Greek translation of the Old Testament, only instead of talking about the works *of Christ*, the Old Testament emphasized the works *of God*, or works *of the Lord*. For example, Psa 111:2 says, "Great are the works of the Lord, studied by all who delight in them."[19] John, in his writings, records Jesus' speaking often of the Father's works and the significance of his own works. Before healing a man born blind, Jesus said "It was not that this man sinned, or his parents, but that the *works of God* might be displayed in him" (John 9:3, emphasis added). In John ten, Jesus responded to the Jews who had picked up stones to stone him, "I have shown you many *good works from the Father*; for which of them are you going to stone me?" (John 10:32, emphasis added). In John fourteen, Jesus explained, "the Father who dwells in me does *his works*" (John 14:10, emphasis added). As the gospels record what Jesus began to do, Scripture calls these his works. As we think about the works of Christ, which were the works of God the Father, it leads us to consider, what does the Old Testament say God the Father is doing? What are the works of God in the Old Testament?

CHAPTER TWO: THE WORKS OR MISSION OF GOD

The verse seemed to jump off the page at me. "Great are the works of the LORD, studied by all who delight in them" (Psa 111:2). Not only does the verse lead the reader to praise the LORD for his great works, but also informs us that if we delight in his works, we will study them. That first epiphany moment, while reading Psalm 111, happened many years ago, but since that time it has seemed wise to **study God's word and his works**. Of course, just because I might think something is a work of God doesn't necessarily mean it is. Those things which the word of God identifies as a work of God are unmistakably so. Since God's word is a perfect treasure and our understanding of his works is not, his word takes priority over our understanding of what should be considered his works. But the Psalm is still clear: his works **are** great, and they **are studied** by all who delight in them. If I am one who delights in what God does, I will study his works. Near the end of Revelation, John describes God being praised for his works, "Great and marvelous are Your works, O Lord God, the Almighty; Righteous and true are Your ways, King of the nations!" (Rev 15:3, NASB). God's works are great and marvelous, and he is to be praised for them.

Jesus modeled studying or paying attention to God's works. After healing the man at the Pool of Bethesda on the Sabbath, Jesus was challenged by the Jews. As he responded to their complaints, Jesus provided us an insight into how he approached life and gave us an example of how we should also approach life. "So Jesus said to them, 'Truly, truly, I say to you, the Son can do nothing of his own accord, but only what he sees the Father doing. For whatever the Father does, that the Son does likewise'" (John 5:19). Jesus first sees what the Father is doing, and then joins in on it. The similarity of seeing what the Father is doing, as Jesus described it, and studying the LORD 's works, as the psalmist put it, connect Jesus' approach to life with the psalm. Studying God's works and joining in on what he is involved in provides an insight into good things to be involved in. In the Old Testament, God is involved in a wide variety of things.

God created the heavens and the earth and, with his first words to Adam and Eve, charged human beings with being stewards of the planet (Gen 1:28), which was described as the work of God in the following chapter. "And on the seventh day God finished his work[20] that he had done" (Gen 2:2). In Psalm 104 the Lord is praised for his works, "O Lord, how manifold are your *works*![21] In wisdom have you made them all; the earth is full of your creatures... These all look to you, to give them their food in due season" (Psa 104:24, 27). Earlier in Psalm 104, past tense verbs were used to describe God's creation: "He set the earth on its foundations... You covered it with the deep... The mountains rose, the valleys sank down... You set a boundary that they may not pass" (Psa 104:5-9). But then the Psalmist switched to present tense verbs to describe the Lord's ongoing care of creation: "You make springs gush forth in the valleys... they give drink to every beast of the field... you water the mountains; the earth is satisfied with the fruit of your work. You cause the grass to grow for the livestock and plants for man to cultivate that he may bring forth food from the earth" (Psa 104:10-14). The phrase "you water the mountains" provides a fascinating insight into what the Scriptures consider the works of God. The verse clearly refers to the rain that comes down on the mountains, the ongoing, present tense means of watering the earth. Based on Job thirty-six we have every reason to believe that people in Job's day, many centuries before the psalmist, had a clear picture of the rain cycle!

Behold, God is great, and we know him not;
the number of his years is unsearchable.
For he draws up the drops of water;
they distill his mist in rain,
which the skies pour down
and drop on mankind abundantly (Job 36:26-28).

Here is a picture of water being drawn up into the clouds to come down again in rain. Henry Morris (whose Ph.D. was in hydraulic engineering and was former chair of the Department of Civil Engineering at Virginia Tech University) lists this passage among "several significant references in Job that are remarkably consistent with modern hydrology and meteorology."[22] God's works do not just refer to the extraordinary, or miraculous events on earth. God, as the all-wise Creator, is the author of all natural laws, when correctly understood.

The same theme of God watering the earth is found in Psa 65:9, but with a different introduction.

"You visit (or "care for")[23] the earth and water it;
you greatly enrich it;
the river of God is full of water;
you provide their grain,
for so you have prepared it.

God's watering the earth is part of his "care for the earth." Care for the earth is one of the works of God. All who are involved in care for the earth in a positive way are lining up with one of the works of God.

Scripture always maintains the balance that human beings are to rule over the earth and are never to worship it or serve it. In Deuteronomy four, Moses warned against worshipping or serving the creation. "And beware lest you raise your eyes to heaven, and when you see the sun and the moon and the stars, all the host of heaven, you be drawn away and bow down to [worship] them and serve them" (Deut 4:19). Rom 1:25 describes a situation where God gave people over to impurity: "They exchanged the truth about God for a lie, and worshiped and served created things [or creation[24]] rather than the Creator—who is forever praised. Amen" (NIV). God's works include provision for all animals and food for people! As human beings, and particularly as believers, work to care for creation they are joining in the works of God, from one perspective, which rightfully should lead to praising the Creator of creation. Whenever human beings make creation their ultimate purpose or passion, in the place of the Creator of creation, they have exchanged the truth for a lie and have moved into worshipping and serving creation. As we consider the works of God in the Old Testament, one of God's works is creation and creation care.

Moses taught the children of Israel that the LORD their God "executes justice for the fatherless and the widow, and loves the sojourner, giving him food and clothing" (Deut 10:18). While partial to orphans and widows, justice is central to what the Lord does. Psa 9:7-9 states, "But the LORD sits enthroned forever; he has established his throne for justice, and he judges the world with righteousness; he judges the peoples with uprightness. The LORD is a stronghold for the oppressed, a stronghold in times of trouble." The reason he established his throne was for justice. The scope of his concern for justice is seen in Psa 103:6, "The LORD works righteousness and justice for all who are oppressed." In Jer 51:10 the LORD is praised for his vindication of the oppressed: "The LORD has brought about our vindication; come, let us declare in Zion the work of the LORD our God."[25] When God judges the wicked, "Then all mankind fears; they tell what God has brought about and ponder what he has done" (Psa 64:9). The theme of justice is repeated in Isaiah, "But the LORD of hosts is exalted in justice, and the Holy God shows himself holy in righteousness" (Isa 5:16). In the first Servant Song, the Messiah "will not grow faint or be discouraged till he has established justice in the earth; and the coastlands wait for his law" (Isa 42:4). When the prophet Micah wrote the summary statement of what the Lord requires of human beings, justice was

24

central because that is who God is and what he does. "He has told you, O man, what is good; and what does the LORD require of you but to do justice, and to love kindness, and to walk humbly with your God" (Mic 6:8). Working for justice on the earth is a way to join in one of God's works.

The Lord's concern for justice and the helpless starts very early in life. The creation of the first human beings was part of God's work of creation, "So God created man in his own image, in the image of God he created him; male and female he created them." It was the work of God that created human beings as male or female. Psalm 139 makes very clear that God is also at work in the formation of every human life in the mother's womb. "For you formed my inward parts; you knitted me together in my mother's womb. I praise you, for I am fearfully and wonderfully made. Wonderful are your works; my soul knows it very well" (Psa 139:13-14). Adam is not the author, but David, who lived long after Adam. God's wonderful works involve the knitting together of every human life! In our desire to study God's working and to consider how to join him, the life of the unborn is an unmistakable work of God. Consequently, every project to improve the well-being of pregnant women across the world, or the well-being of newborns, is a way to join God in his work. Every effort to protect the safety of unborn human beings is a way to join God in his work. Not only does the Old Testament commend those who study God's works, God speaks against those who do not regard his works. "Because they do not regard the works of the Lord nor the deeds of His hands, He will tear them down and not build them up" (Psa 28:5). The matter of working with, and not against, the Lord is a serious matter! Every culture that fails to protect the unborn is acting contrary to the "wonderful... works" (Psa 139:14) of God.

Continuing with the broad-brush stroke that describes God's works, Psa 145:9 states "The LORD is good to all, And His mercies are over all

His works" (NASB). Whenever people show mercy, they are working in line with the works of God! Mercy ministries are applied to many areas of needs in the world, and they are one way of joining in God's work!

Much like Jesus was involved in a number of different things in the gospels, the works of God the Father touch much of life. The overview of Luke's gospel and the use of God's works have prepared us to think about the broad work of God. Beginning in the mid 1900s, the term Mission of God (*missio Dei*) became central in discussions of missions, the church, God, and salvation. The term became so broad as to include all that God is doing in the world, or as David Bosch stated, "God's activity, which embraces both the church and the world, and in which the church may be privileged to participate."[26] Perhaps the term comes close to the Old Testament concept of "the works of the Lord." God is at work in our world for justice. God is at work in the world caring for the planet. God is at work in the world providing food for the hungry. God is at work in the world forming every new human being. God is at work in the world showing mercy.

As believers, we desire to study God's works and join him at work. The works of God or the mission of God includes food for the hungry and when a Christian gets involved in giving food to the hungry that Christian can be said to be living missionally.[27] They are living consistent with, or in a manner related to, God's working or God's mission. Because God is involved in watering the planet to provide food for animals, to the degree that a person, particularly a Christian, is a good steward of the planet and provides clean water or cares for needy animals, in the biggest picture that person is living consistent with the works of God, consistent with the mission of God, which could be called living missionally. Because every unborn child is an unborn human being and is knit together in the mother's womb by a loving, heavenly Father, every person who provides care for the unborn or speaks up and advocates for the unborn is lining up with the wonderful works of God, lining up with God's mission which could be described as living missionally.

In this broad sense, the "works of God" (a very biblical term) can be called the activity of God or the mission of God. The activity of God is very diverse. However, the Scriptures do not leave such a broad-brush stroke as they describe the working of God in the world. Yes, without question God is at work in all the ways described. However, there is a focus to his working, according to Jesus. There is an overarching story through Scripture and through human history.

CHAPTER THREE: WHEN JESUS OPENED THEIR UNDERSTANDING

We are considering how the Scriptures would have us place "missionaries in the mission of God." The opening two verses of Acts provide hints at how the whole of Scripture might address the issue. Luke began the second volume of his two-volume history pointing back to the first book, pointing back with a precise overview statement of The Gospel According to Luke. "In the first book, O Theophilus, I have dealt with all that Jesus began to do and teach," which points us to the works of God or the mission of God. The next verse refers to "the apostles whom he had chosen," which will allow us to discuss the work of missionaries in that mission.

In chapter one we walked through Luke's gospel to remind us specifically of what Jesus did and taught, recognizing that he has not stopped doing or teaching those things. There was a certain breadth to the things that Jesus did and taught. Following the resurrection, Jesus had pointed out to the two on the road to Emmaus, and then to all his disciples, that he had personally prophesied that he would die and rise again, but also that the Old Testament had also foretold the same. However, Jesus had not simply pointed to a few prophecies of the cross or resurrection. Jesus opened the disciples' minds to understand the overview of, the outline of, the major topics of, the key to the understanding of the Scriptures.[28] "Then he opened their minds to understand the Scriptures, and said to them, "Thus it is written, that the Christ should suffer and on the third day rise from the dead, and that repentance for the forgiveness of sins should be proclaimed in his name to all nations, beginning from Jerusalem" (Luke 24:25-27). What Jesus began to do and teach was not left in broad strokes by Luke in the gospel. Actually, God's working in the Old Testament, as well as all of Scripture, is not scattered or random. God's working, or the mission of God, as revealed in Scripture has a dual focus: the Messiah and the missionary task.

Earlier on Resurrection Day, Jesus had appeared to the two walking on the road to Emmaus. He began with a question, as was his custom, about the topic of their conversation. The question brought out their description of the rejection of Jesus and his death on the cross, but also helped them voice that they had been hoping that Jesus would have been the promised Messiah, "the one to redeem Israel" (Luke 24:21). They recounted the confusing report of the women who said the tomb was empty and the angel who "said that he was alive" (Luke 24:23). Their colleagues had gone and found the tomb empty. Jesus then gently called them "foolish ones, and slow of heart" because they had only believed part of the Old Testament promises, the part about the Messiah's reign. They had been slow "to believe *all* that the prophets have spoken!" (Luke 24:25, emphasis added). As Norval Geldenhuys explains,

> If they had known the Scriptures and really believed in the living God, they would have known that not only had the glory of victory been promised Him as Messiah in the Old Testament, *but that God had clearly proclaimed through the prophets that He was to suffer and to die and thus to attain to glory.*[29]

They had correctly seen the prophecies of the reigning Messiah in the Old Testament. But the Old Testament also told of the way to his reign, the path that would lead to glory. If they had understood "all that the prophets have spoken," the rest of the Old Testament prophecies, they would have been better prepared for the events of the last days. Then, "beginning with

Moses and all the Prophets, he interpreted to them in all the Scriptures the things concerning himself" (Luke 24:27).

We are not told which passages Jesus used or how he interpreted them, but he started with Moses. Perhaps Jesus gave an overview of sacrifices in the Old Testament, going back to the garden, to the protoevangelium, the first telling of the good news, "I will put enmity between you and the woman, and between your offspring and her offspring; he shall bruise your head, and you shall bruise his heel" (Gen 3:15). God then provided animal skins to cover Adam and Eve, often speculated to be a lamb killed for each person (Gen 3:21). Perhaps Jesus told of Abraham's confession that "God will provide himself a lamb" for Isaac his son (Gen 22:8, KJV). Then there were in Exodus the families who had slain "a lamb for a household" (Exo 12:3), put the blood of the lamb over the door, and when the Lord saw the blood he would pass over that house (Exo 12:13). Or the Day of Atonement when once a year the lamb was killed for the sins of the nation (Lev 16:17). As Tom Elliff describes it, "first, in the Garden of Eden, there was a lamb for a man. In Egypt, the sacrifice was a lamb for a family. Then, in the wilderness of Sinai, the sacrifice was of a lamb for a nation. God was preparing mankind for the day when, in the fullness of time, there would be sacrificed a lamb for the world."[30] Perhaps Jesus provided an overview for Cleopas and his companion of the sacrifices of the Old Testament pointing to "the Lamb of God who takes away the sin of the world!" (John 1:29).

While Luke does not record in chapter twenty-four any details about how Jesus interpreted the Scriptures to them, Luke does record in the book of Acts the passages about the cross used by the apostles and their disciples. In Acts eight, deacon Philip came upon the Ethiopian eunuch reading Isa 53:7-8, about the crucifixion.

> "Like a sheep he was led to the slaughter
> and like a lamb before its shearer is silent,

so he opens not his mouth.
In his humiliation justice was denied him.
Who can describe his generation?
For his life is taken away from the earth."

Perhaps Jesus had started earlier in Isaiah 53 to talk about the cross, "He was despised and rejected by men; a man of sorrows and acquainted with grief… But he was pierced for our transgressions… All we like sheep have gone astray; we have turned—every one—to his own way; and the Lord has laid on him the iniquity of us all" (Isa 53:3-6). Jesus had spoken to the two on the road to Emmaus from Moses and the prophets about the cross.

Following Peter's confession that Jesus was the Christ, Jesus had carefully and repeatedly taught the disciples that the Scriptures had foretold that he was going to die and that three days later he was going to rise from the dead (Luke 9:22, 44; 18:31-34; 24:7). Perhaps, on the afternoon of resurrection day, he had shared with Cleopas and his friend passages from the Old Testament about the resurrection. In the second chapter of Acts, Luke provides details of Peter's sermon, preached not long afterwards, where Peter quotes from Psalm sixteen about the resurrection. "For you will not abandon my soul to Hades, or let your Holy One see corruption. You have made known to me the paths of life; you will make me full of gladness with your presence" (Acts 2:27-28; Psa 16:10-11). Peter then interprets the psalm, that David "foresaw and spoke about *the resurrection of the Christ*, that he was not abandoned to Hades, nor did his flesh see corruption. This Jesus God raised up, and of that we all are witnesses" (Acts 2:31-32, emphasis added). Perhaps we have an idea about what Jesus said that day as we consider what his disciples later repeated about his resurrection. Jesus may have turned to the promises of a prophet like Moses who would come (Deut 18:15; Acts 3:22) or of a descendant of David whose reign would never end (Isa 9:6-7; Acts 2:30). Whatever he shared, "they said to each other, 'Did not our hearts burn within us while he talked to us on the road, while he opened to us the Scriptures?'" (Luke 24:32).

Later that evening, Jesus shared with the eleven.[31] One wonders if Jesus shared some of the same things with the apostles that he had shared earlier with the two travelers. After assuring them it was really him with the offer to touch his hands and feet, and with the demonstration of eating fish, Jesus reminded them he had foretold these events previously. The things written about him in the Scriptures had to be fulfilled. Perhaps he related some of the content from the road to Emmaus.

Then something else happens. Like verse forty-four, verse forty-five begins with "then." After he reminded them that he had often spoken to them of the prophesies of his death and resurrection on the third day, then he added something amazing. Then..., then the risen Lord "opened their minds to understand the Scriptures!" (Luke 24:45). This is not a great prophet. This is not a great teacher. This is not a wonderful pastor or preacher. This is none other than the risen Lord, God incarnate! Verses forty-six and forty-seven provide *Jesus'* outline of Scripture, Jesus' overview of Scripture, Jesus' key to "understand Scriptures." Much like the first half of the gospel closed with the crescendo of the Transfiguration clearly identifying Jesus as the Lord of Glory, Luke brings the entire gospel to a close with the crescendo of Jesus explaining the storyline of history! As John in the Revelation saw that only the Lion who was the Lamb could open the scroll (Rev 5:1-5), Luke gives us the risen Lord's explanation that will open our minds today.

"Thus it is written, that the Christ should suffer and on the third day rise from the dead, and that repentance for the forgiveness of sins should be proclaimed in his name to all nations, beginning from Jerusalem" (Luke 24:46-47).

"Thus it is written" or "this is what is written in Scripture" (CSB, NIV). This is the focus of all that was written in the Old Testament. This is the storyline of the Old Testament. "The Christ should suffer and on the third day rise from the dead." The first part of the outline of Scripture deals with *the Messiah*, and specifically his death and resurrection. (The first volume of Luke's history had unpacked that Jesus was the Messiah and he chose to suffer on the cross and was raised the third day.) Secondly, "repentance for the forgiveness of sins should be proclaimed in his name to all nations, beginning from Jerusalem." The second part of the outline of Scripture is *the missionary task*: repentance that leads to forgiveness of sins, made possible by the Christ's death and resurrection, is to be proclaimed in his name to all nations. (Luke concentrated his second volume on showing how the gospel, with the call to repent, was preached to the nations.)[32] In light of the fact that all human beings will spend eternity in heaven with their Creator, or else separated from him for eternity, based on this proclamation (and their subsequent response to it), the second half of Jesus' explanation is a focus on what will decide human beings' eternity!

Jesus' short explanation included "forgiveness of sins," dealt with the source of what's wrong with our world, dealt with sin. The promised Messiah was God's answer to what has gone wrong with the world, to the problem of sin. The key to understanding the Scriptures must include the idea of sin, must answer the question of what has gone wrong in the world. The storyline of Scripture begins with Creator God creating a world and a universe where "everything that he had made... was very good" (Gen 1:31). Revelation twenty-one and twenty-two make clear that history is moving to a place where all will be made right again. But between the book ends of Genesis one and two and Revelation twenty-one and twenty-two, something is very wrong. What is the answer for what is wrong in our world?

It is true that at the end of creation all was good. However, the first man and woman, created in the very image of God, chose to rebel against, chose to take the place of, God—chose to sin. Why is the world we live in

34

broken? Why is all creation groaning (Rom 8:22)? Because of human beings' choice to rebel against the good Creator! However, instead of that rebellion ending the story, God mercifully called out to Adam and Eve in the cool of the garden, provided a sacrifice, a covering for them, and promised that one would come, the seed of the woman, who would crush the enemy. The first three chapters of Genesis follow the same outline provided by Jesus. God created a good world, by sin human beings marred that world. But God promised one to come. God refused to let sin win.

The first epoch of human history, from Genesis one through eleven, continued to show how sinful, not just Adam and Eve, but all who followed them were. In the first family, after Cain killed his brother Abel, God reaches out to Cain, who then went away from the Lord's presence. God graciously gave Adam and Eve another son, Seth. The world became so very wicked that the Creator judged his creation (Gen 6:5-7). God had made it. It was his to judge. But again, he graciously provided escape. Noah constructed the ark and preached. Of all who heard the message, only eight entered the ark and were saved from the penalty of death that came because of sin. At the Tower of Babel human beings continued to try to take the place of God, continued to rebel against him. Perhaps chapter eleven ends without a gracious resolution, except for the introduction of a seventy-five-year-old man, "as good as dead" (Heb 11:12), named Abram, and his barren wife Sarai (Gen 11:30; 12:4).[33]

The second epoch of human history stretched from Abraham to David and found the same pattern of God's goodness, man's sin, and God's refusal to let sin win. God's call to Abraham introduces more details of Jesus' description of Scripture.

> Now the LORD said to Abram, "Go from your country and your kindred and your father's house to the land that I will show you. And I will make of you a great nation, and I will bless you and make your name great, so that you will be a blessing. I will bless those who bless you, and him who

dishonors you I will curse, and in you all the families of the earth shall be blessed" (Gen 12:1-3).

God's plan was for "all the families of the earth." Just as he had created all and had judged all, he explicitly promises blessings for all the families of the earth. Jesus spoke of proclaiming forgiveness "to all nations." Abraham's call spoke of blessing on "all the families of the earth." As God continues to unpack Abraham's call over the coming years, he specifies that it is through Abraham's seed that all the nations of the earth will be blessed (Gen 22:18). Paul makes clear that the promised seed is none other than the Christ (Gal 3:16), the first half of Jesus' outline in Luke twenty-four about the Messiah, the promised seed of Abraham. From Abraham, God formed the nation Israel giving them the Law of Moses and the promised land. The law clarified God's standards to make clear that no one can keep them, bringing the "knowledge of sin" (Rom 3:20). The law also specified endless sacrifices for sin. The message was clear: all humans sin (Lev 4:13; Psa 14:1-3; Rom 3:23), the payment for sin is death, but another can pay the price as a substitute (Lev 4:15; Rom 6:23) that leads to forgiveness (Lev 4:20; Rom 10:9). The wonderful news of forgiveness based on substitutionary death was marred because "it is impossible for the blood of bulls and goats to take away sins" (Heb 10:4) or else they would "have ceased to be offered" (Heb 10:2). The period from Abraham to David pointed to the need for one who would suffer for sin and then crush the head of the enemy by being victorious over sin!

The third epoch of the Old Testament began with David.[34] During the reign of David and Solomon, the nation of Israel was firmly established, it ruled over the surrounding nations, and the temple was built. However, the ugly head of sin continued to be seen with David's unfaithfulness and Solomon's worshipping other gods. The promise of a descendant of David, the Messiah who would reign forever (2 Sam 7:16; Isa 9:7) captured the hope of the nation, perhaps even obscuring the many passages that foretold of his suffering and death (case in point, the two on the road to Emmaus). The nation continued in sin while prophets, an occasional godly king, and more prophets called them back to God but also continued to foretell the Messiah's coming (Isa 9:6-7; Jer 31:31-32; Ezek 36:22-23; Dan 7:13-14; Hos 2:19-20; Joel 2:28-32; Mic 5:2; Nah 2:15; Hab 2:4; Hag 2:9; Zech 9:9; 11:12-13; 12:10; 13:7; 14:4, 9). In this third epoch, Jesus' second emphasis on preaching repentance to all nations begins to become clearer in Scripture. It is true, Abraham's covenant unmistakably called for blessing on all the families of the earth, but the people of God had rejected his invitation to be a kingdom of priests (Exod 20:19—Heb 12:25).[35]

The psalms clearly recognized that God blesses his people so "that your way may be known on earth, your saving power among all nations. Let the peoples praise you, O God; let all the peoples praise you!" (Psa 67:2-3). They call for his people to "Make known His deeds among the peoples" (Psa 105:1) and to, "Tell of His glory among the nations" (Psa 96:3) so that, "All the kings of the earth shall give you thanks, O Lord, for they have heard the words of your mouth, and they shall sing of the ways of the Lord, for great is the glory of the Lord" (Psa 138:4). The heart of God is to, "Let the nations be glad and sing for joy" (Psa 67:4).

The prophets not only spoke of the Messiah's suffering and triumph, but also of the good news going to all nations. "How beautiful upon the mountains are the feet of him who brings good news" (Isa 52:7) so that "all the ends of the earth shall see the salvation of our God" (Isa 52:10). As William Carey highlighted, the LORD called for his people to, "Enlarge the place of your tent... for you will spread abroad to the right and to the left, and your offspring will possess the nations" (Isa 54:2-3). The LORD was not just the God of one nation, but the "Holy one of Israel is your Redeemer, the God of the whole earth he is called" (Isa 54:5). The prophets foretold the day when, "the foreigners who join themselves to the LORD, to minister to him, to love the name of the Lord and to be his servants... these I will bring to my holy mountain... for my house shall be called a house of prayer for all peoples" (Isa 56:6-7). The LORD offers "Peace, peace, to the far and to the near" (Isa 57:19—Eph 2:17); and that, "the time is coming to gather all nations and tongues... And from them I will send survivors to the nations... to the coastlands far away, that have not heard my fame or seen my glory. And they shall declare my glory among the nations. And they shall bring all your brothers from all the nations as an offering to the Lord... And some of them also I will take for priests and for Levites, says the Lord" (Isa 66:18-21). All through the Old Testament, God's concern was for all the earth, He identified Himself as the God of all the earth. He is the rightful Lord of every nation on earth. In truth, he is not a foreign God anywhere on the planet but is their Creator, only Savior, and rightful Lord! However, the nations need to have the good news preached to them!

Jesus opened their minds to understand the Scriptures and said that what was written had this focus, what was written could be outlined like this, what was written could be summarized like this, The Messiah and the missionary task. The message of the Old Testament is that human beings have all sinned and are separated from God. He sent the Messiah to pay the price for that sin and to triumph over it by his resurrection on the third day. The good news of God's solution to human beings' problem is to be proclaimed among the nations offering forgiveness of sins to those who will repent. That's what the Old Testament is about. But that is also what the New Testament is about! Actually, from the perspective of eternity, *that is what all human history is about!*

Scripture makes a clear distinction between what is temporary and what is eternal. And in Scripture, temporary doesn't necessarily mean a few hours, days, weeks, years, centuries, or millennium. As the writer of Hebrews begins his work, in chapter one he establishes the supremacy of the Son of God. In verse eight he establishes that the psalmist said of the

Son, "Your throne, O God, is forever and ever." He then shows the uniqueness of his eternal reign in contrast to creation by quoting from Psalm 102. The connection is extremely significant for our discussion.

"You, Lord, laid the foundation of the earth in the beginning,
and the heavens are the work[36] of your hands;
they will perish, but you remain;
they will all wear out like a garment,
like a robe you will roll them up,
like a garment they will be changed.
But you are the same,
and your years will have no end" (Heb 1:10-12).

The creation of the heavens and earth are the topic. As old as they are, Scripture says, "they will perish, but you remain." Early in this psalm the writer is reflecting on the brevity of his own life. F. F. Bruce notes the psalmist thinking of the creation as lasting much longer than a human being's physical life. "In comparison with his own short life, heaven and earth are long-lived; yet heaven and earth must pass away."[37] However, there is something that lasts much longer than the heaven and earth.

The contrast in duration of the creation to the Son is like a garment of clothing. A favorite piece of clothing is greatly valued. If someone special gave it to you, you enjoy it. *You take care of it*. But it will not last forever. Using the picture of a robe, "you will roll them up, like a garment they will be changed." As David L. Allen makes clear, "The point of contrast in vv. 11—12 is the *perishability of the universe* against the eternality of the Son, hence the simile of the worn out, rolled up garment... The point of the quotation is to stress the *impermanence of creation* as contrasted with the eternality of the Son."[38] However, before the analogy, Hebrews 1:10 says the Lord laid the foundation of the heavens and the earth. The heavens and the earth are the work of his hands. In verse eleven, we are clearly told that the heavens and the earth "will perish... they will wear out." In contrast, speaking of God the Son, "but you remain... your years will have no end." This passage is extremely significant because it specifically names creation, the heavens and the earth, and contrasts their duration to One who is eternal. While creation is to be cared for because of God's command and to line up with God's works, Hebrews one contrasts creation to that which is eternal. This contrast is consistent in Scripture and is something believers are supposed to pay attention to.

Paul writes, "So we fix our eyes not on what is seen, but on what is unseen, since what is seen is temporary, but what is unseen is eternal" (2 Cor 4:18, NIV). We are to recognize what is temporary and what is eternal, and then to adjust our focus based on that fact. We are those who "fix our eyes," who focus on what is unseen because it is eternal. Rick Warren points to the difference it makes to recognize what is eternal, "When you realize life on Earth is just temporary, it radically alters your values. Eternal values, not temporal ones, become the deciding factor for your decisions."[39] God is involved in so many good things and it is legitimate to join him in his works. God distinguishes between what is temporary and what is eternal. His focus in the Old Testament, in the New Testament, and in all human history is on the eternal. Because of their choice to sin (Eph 2:1), human beings are on their path to a horrible eternity separated from God (2 Thess 1:8-9; John 3:36; Matt 25:46). While doing many good things, God's focus is on the Messiah who would die for human beings' sin and the proclamation of forgiveness in his name to all.

Jesus modeled doing and teaching many good things, and all of them are valid things for believers to be involved in. The works of God, in Christ and in the Old Testament, include a variety of things. It is positive for all people to invest their time and resources in things that are consistent with what God is doing. However, Scripture provides a framework for all such activity. It is very appropriate to care for the planet, while continually remembering the planet is not eternal but every human being will spend eternity in one of two eternal places. That knowledge keeps anyone from

40

worshipping or putting undo value in caring for creation instead of seeking and worshipping the Creator. Working for justice in any setting is beautifully consistent with the character of God. However, injustice is not eternal. Wise workers for justice will always keep in mind what is eternal. It is wonderful to have compassion for the hungry and feed them like Jesus did. However, hunger is not eternal. Poverty is not eternal. Homelessness is not eternal. Mental illness is not eternal. Sickness is not eternal. Heaven, hell, and the souls of people are eternal! All the mission of God, the works of God, are valid but should be seen through Jesus' explanation of the overarching story. All the mission of God invites human beings to join him, but the biblical way to do that is by doing those things with eternity in focus.

CHAPTER FOUR: GIFTS, GOD'S PREPARATION FOR YOUR PARTICIPATION

The summary of Luke's first volume in the two-volume church history fascinates for its breadth and for its timeline. Luke explains that what he dealt with in his gospel was "all that Jesus began to do and teach." Our walk through the gospel confirmed a wide range of things that Jesus did and taught. The idea that the gospel was just what Jesus *began* to do and teach suggested that he has continued to do those things through his body, the church. As believers, that insight presents a very broad list of things in which we could get involved, of things to which we could dedicate our lives, ways we could join Jesus at work. Then in the Old Testament we found a similar breadth of the works of God, or what could be called the mission of God. But the closing paragraphs of Luke brought a focus to the broad activities. The mission of God in Scripture is quite broad, but the central message of the Scriptures, God's focus of history, has to do with the Messiah and the missionary task. While God is still the master of all the broad list of things, we find him doing in Scripture, He says He is doing those things with a focus. Up to this point, we have painted a picture of many, many things that believers can get involved in, so long as they do those things with eternity in focus. In this chapter, we are going to add another biblical truth that helps believers know how to join God in his mission. At the moment of repenting and believing in Jesus, the Holy Spirit came to live inside every believer and as he did, each believer received certain spiritual gifts. Gifts are like God preparing you to participate in his mission.

Spiritual gifts are an important way that every Christian is prepared to be actively involved in what God is doing through the church. On the topic of spiritual gifts, Paul explained to the Corinthians that the Holy Spirit "distributes them to each one, just as he determines. Just as a body, though one, has many parts, but all its many parts form one body, so it is with Christ. For we were all baptized by one Spirit so as to form one body— whether Jews or Gentiles, slave or free —and we were all given the one Spirit to drink" (1 Cor 12:11-13, NIV). Since Paul can say to the believers at Corinth, "we were all baptized by one Spirit" then we can say that all Christians have been, in the past, at the moment of conversion, baptized by the Holy Spirit. This means that at the moment of salvation every believer was placed into the body of Christ, the universal church,[40] and the Holy Spirit came to live inside of them. The Holy Spirit moreover chose which spiritual gift you would have, because he "distributes them to each one just as he determines."

Paul likewise wrote to the church at Rome about spiritual gifts. He said that some are gifted to encourage (Rom 12:8). Now we know that every Christian is commanded to encourage one another (1 Thess 5:11), but some are just really good at it, some are gifted by God as encouragers. We know that every believer is commanded to serve one another (Gal 5:13), but some are given the spiritual gift of service (Rom 12:7). They find great satisfaction in serving. They are affirmed by the body of Christ when they have served. They just seem to be good at serving. Hebrews 5:12 says, "For though by this time you ought to be teachers," so we know that all believers are to teach in some way. But we also know that there are some who are just gifted as teachers (Rom 12:7). When they teach, the rest of the group says, "Now I get it!" It is just easy for them to clarify what a passage of Scripture means. We know that Jesus gave the Great

44

Commission to every believer and, as they go through life, they are to make disciples, particularly of other groups or ethnicities. However, in 1 Cor 12:29, Paul asks a rhetorical question with an assumed answer of "no." "All are not apostles, are they?" (NASB). Even though every Christian is given the Great Commission, not every Christian must leave their home and family and move to another place to plant churches like Paul did, like missionaries do.[41] We know that all believers are to "go home to your friends and tell how" God has worked in their lives (Mark 5:19). However, Eph 5:11 says that God put some people in the body as evangelists. They are just good at seeing opportunities to share the gospel during the day and how to turn ordinary conversations to the gospel. By the way, Ephesians five also says that part of what evangelists are supposed to do, in addition to evangelizing, is to equip the rest of the body to be able to share better!

With these examples of what spiritual gifts look like, let's return to our passage in 1 Corinthians 12 to think about how the idea of spiritual gifts helps believers to know how they fit into God's mission. These gifts fit together into the body of Christ. "Just as a body, though one, has many parts, but all its many parts form one body, so it is with Christ" (1 Cor 12:11). The idea of a body having many parts points to the diversity of the body of Christ. While we are very grateful that our body has a stomach, we are grateful we do not have only stomachs underneath our skin. Something must pump the blood! The diversity of gifts in the body of Christ highlights how different Christians' gifts are to complement others and work together. The description of spiritual gifts as making up a body also suggests how believers fit into the mission of God. It is very healthy for ever believer to think about how they are gifted spiritually. Some simple steps can help with this process. Pray for God to show you what gift he has given you. Study what the Bible says about spiritual gifts. Take advantage of God-given opportunities to become involved in a variety of different ministries and then evaluate how well each one was a fit for you.

Ask other believers to share how they see you being most effective in the body of Christ.

Once you have some idea about what spiritual gift or gifts you may have, this provides an interesting starting point to see where to join in the works of God. If one part of the human body is good at holding things and another part is good at making sounds, perhaps the first should think about serving as a hand and the second as a mouth. Similarly, if your gift is teaching, you take advantage of opportunities to teach. If your gift is service, you sign up for projects that need service. If your gift is encouragement, you don't worry if you are spending lots of time visiting with people who are discouraged. That's how you build up the body! Knowing your spiritual gift helps you know how to fit into the mission of God. However, knowing your spiritual gift does not excuse any believer from being an obedient follower of Christ.

GIFTS AND COMMANDS

While every believer has unique gifts that prepare them to fit into the works of God, every believer is to obey every command found in the New Testament that pertains to all Christians. Like spiritual gifts are God's preparation for us to join him, his commands can be seen as invitations to join him at work. The New Testament contains several "one another" passages that make body-life wonderful inside the church. No Christian is exempt from being obedient. We are all to "love one another" (John 13:34); "Be devoted to one another in brotherly love" (Rom 12:10, NASB); "Through love serve one anther" (Gal 5:13); "Bear one another's burdens, and so fulfill the law of Christ" (Gal 6:2); "Be kind to one another, tender-hearted, forgiving one another, just as God in Christ forgave you" (Eph 4:32); "Do not lie to one another, seeing that you have put off the old self with its practices" (Col 3:9); "Therefore encourage one another and build one another up, just as you are doing" (1 Thess 5:11).

What a wonderful blessing to be a part of a church that acts like this! (If you have experienced something different in a church, please allow me to apologize. But please know, that was not how God designed church!)

The 'one another' passages are not optional to some Christians because they are commands. All believers do other things just because they are Christ-like. Remember every Christian can say, "I have been crucified with Christ. It is no longer I who live, but Christ who lives in me. And the life I now live in the flesh I live by faith in the Son of God, who loved me and gave himself for me" (Gal 2:20). Christians do not minister to the poor just because they think they have some gift, they do so because they are Christ-like. Christians are not excused from serving just because their gift is teaching, they do it because Christ does it through them. Being filled with the Spirit means I am under his influence, and he produces in me the fruit of the Spirit and lives the Christ-life through me.

There are also commands that are personal, you are guided by the Holy Spirit to do a certain thing even though it is not a command in the New Testament. For you, it is not optional. While the commands in Scripture have the advantage of being in black and white, and guidance by the Spirit is subject to my misunderstanding, I am still called to obey. Jesus said, "My sheep hear my voice, and I know them, and they follow me" (John 10:27). What an amazing truth that the God of Glory, the Risen Lord, has such a personal relationship with us that he said we hear his voice! For some biblical examples, when Paul and Silas began the second missionary journey, they had planned to go to Asia minor, but they were "forbidden by the Holy Spirit to speak the word in Asia" (Acts 16:6). They then they "attempted to go into Bithynia but the Spirit of Jesus did not allow them" (Acts 16:7). We are not told how the Holy Spirit closed these doors and made his will clear, but Paul knew it without mistake. Next came the vision in the night of the man of Macedonia saying, "'Come over to Macedonia and help us.' And when Paul had seen the vision, immediately we sought to go on into Macedonia, concluding that God had called us to preach the gospel to them" (Acts 16:9-10). The Spirit had given specific, personal guidance to the missionary team and they obeyed. Earlier in Acts, Philip was a refugee in Samaria and saw many people saved. God guided him to go to a desert road from Jerusalem to Gaza. When he obeyed, he found a caravan with an Ethiopian official in one chariot. The Bible says, "And the Spirit said to Philip, Go over and join this chariot" (Acts 8:29)! The same God who guided Philip to leave the revival in Samaria and go to a desert road, clearly guided him as to which chariot he was to approach! Again, we are not told how God guided, but Philip knew that it was God and knew what God was telling him to do!

While every believer is to obey all commands given to every believer, it is wise to spend as much time as possible in the middle of your gifts. Unless you are commanded to do something distinct, spending as much time as possible using your spiritual gifts is one way to line up with what God has done in your life. You didn't pick the gift. He did. When you use it, you are being a good steward of what he has given. You are being soft clay in the potter's hands. You are leaning into who God has shaped you to be. There is a clear sense in which your natural talents are also God's gifts, since he knit you together in your mother's womb (Psa 139:13). There is also a sense in which your life experiences have been under his sovereign providence. Your gifts, talents and experiences have all prepared you to fit into God's mission in a way that fits you.

ROLES OR ASSIGNMENTS

Just like spiritual gifts do not excuse any believer from obeying God's commands, by Word or Spirit, sometimes God opens a door for service, a role to fill or an assignment to accept. As we would expect, often the doors God opens for service are in the middle of our spiritual gifts. The role we are asked to fill often uses our gifts. However, this is not always the case.

48

Sometimes we serve best from positions of weakness rather than positions of strength. Remember, God told Paul, "My grace is sufficient for you, for my power is made perfect in weakness" (2 Cor 12:9).

There are times in life when we are asked to take a role or an assignment that may be outside of our gift set. However, with time we see that God was using that time to minister to someone in that place or to prepare us for what he had next for us. It is very encouraging that the Lord of the Harvest is all-wise and all-powerful. We can trust him if he opens a door or guides us to take an assignment.

We have been considering how believers can join the mission of God. God is involved in many things in the world and guides believers to join him in many different ways. Always, we are to do all tasks with eternity in focus, remembering that the outline of Scripture and history is the Messiah and the missionary task. Our spiritual gifts are a good indicator of how we are to join God's working, but they are not the only way. Of course, every Christian does many things because of the commands of Christ and being Christ-like. Also, God opens doors and makes assignments that are opportunities to join him regardless of how he has gifted us. Now, having thought about the mission of God and how believers in general join in God's working, we are ready to look at a particular part of the body of Christ. Let's locate missionaries in the mission of God.

"The Apostles Whom He Had Chosen" Acts 1:2

The opening verses of Acts provide an important connection between the three decades described in the Luke's first volume, dealing with all that Jesus began to do and teach, and the three decades that followed as the church expanded from Jerusalem to the primary city of the world, Rome. An amazing amount of latitude was found as we walked through the gospel and considered the compassionate care Jesus modeled for the hungry and the hurting, for the grieving and the outcast. He established his identity by demonstrating his power over sickness, nature, and even death. He taught us to love one another, to forgive as we have been forgiven, to do unto others as we wish to be done by. He clearly, repeatedly told his followers ahead of time that he was going to Jerusalem, to suffer and die, and then was going to rise from the dead on the third day, just as Scriptures had foretold. Then, he went to Jerusalem, suffered and died, and rose from the dead on the third day, just as Scriptures had foretold! Jesus had said that his works were the works of God, a theme running throughout the Old Testament.

In the Old Testament, the works of God cover perhaps an even broader spectrum than the works of Christ in the New. The works of God specifically include his creation of all that is and his providential care for the earth by sending rain and providing food for the animals. The works of God include his compassion for the fatherless and widows and for all oppressed by injustice. The works of God specifically include his activity in "knitting together" every human being in their mother's womb and his works of mercy. The works of God have a breadth about them that point to all that he is involved in. During the mid-1900s, all that God is involved in came to be called the mission of God.

Both Jesus' ministry and the works of God (or the mission of God) are extensive in scope but are focused, according to God's own explanation. Jesus summarized or focused the Old Testament as being about the Messiah's coming and death, and the proclamation of forgiveness of sins in his name to all nations: the Messiah and the missionary task. However, the New Testament and all human history have the same focus. Believers can join in any of the things Jesus did in the New Testament or any of the works of God in the Old Testament and they are joining God at work, or in other words, participating in the mission of God, so long as they do any of those things with eternity in focus.

God has gifted every believer to join in his work, to fit into the body of Christ, with their spiritual gifts. While spiritual gifts are a primary indicator as to how to be involved, they cannot excuse believers from obeying the commands of God by Word or Spirit, or excuse believers from accepting the roles or assignments they believe God is providing. Since Jesus did not stop doing the things he did or teaching the things he taught, Acts 1:1 provides an invitation for all believers to join God at work, be part of the mission of God. Now, Acts 1:2 introduces a particular part of the body of Christ: apostles.

In the first chapters of Acts, "apostles" only refer to the twelve. One of the twelve, Peter, is the primary human actor in the first half of Acts. However, by the first missionary journey the Holy Spirit working through Luke clearly adds others to the meaning of the word, others who are clearly not part of the twelve but are nonetheless sent-out ones according to the New Testament. These include missionaries today. Paul, who was not one of the twelve, is the primary human actor in the second half of the book. Acts 1:2 introduces the idea of missionaries in the mission of God.[42] These sent-out ones do not change the fact that the Great Commission was given to all believers.[43] However, all can be a part of the sent-out task.[44]

CHAPTER FIVE: THE TWELVE AND SENT-OUT ONES

The unique, closed group of the twelve apostles are described in the opening verses of Acts. Those twelve individuals have died: that group no longer exists. However, others are also included in the New Testament's use of the word apostles. They include sent-out ones who did the same work as missionaries do today.

IDENTITY OF SENT-OUT ONES

The twelve apostles are a very specific group of leaders in redemption history. They are specifically named in the New Testament on four occasions: Matt 10:2-4; Mark 3:16-10; Luke 6:14-16, and lastly in Acts 1:13. Jesus had made clear in Acts 1:2 that he, personally, was the one who had chosen the apostles. At the end of Acts one, after Jesus had left them and before the coming of the Holy Spirit, the eleven name an apostle, even though Jesus had commanded them to wait (Acts 1:4). It is noteworthy that Jesus later did personally name another apostle, his name was Saul of Tarsus or the Apostle Paul.[45] The twelve apostles are such a closed group that in eternity future their names will be on the twelve foundation stones of the New Jerusalem (Rev 21:10, 14). They are not thirteen. They are not fifteen. These twelve are the apostles named in Acts one.

By the first missionary journey, the book of Acts demands that there be a different category that is also called apostles in the New Testament. While the twelve apostles' names are given four times, Barnabas is not on the list. However, the word apostle (or as it could be translated, "sent-out one" or by the Latin-based word "missionary" meaning 'one sent') is unequivocally applied to Barnabas in Acts fourteen. "But when the apostles Barnabas and Paul heard of it, they tore their garments and rushed out into the crowd, crying out" (Acts 14:14). It is fascinating that Barnabas should be the one named as an apostle. He has been in the storyline of Acts since chapter four. We remember that Barnabas was just his nickname, his real name was Joseph. The apostles gave him his nickname, "son of encouragement" (Acts 4:36) because, obviously, he was such an encourager. Remember when Saul of Tarsus had recently been converted and came to Jerusalem. The disciples were extremely skeptical of his conversion because of his background of persecuting the church. It was Barnabas who came along side[46] Paul and spoke up for him to the apostles. The encourager connected the new guy to the right people. When there was a discussion about bringing John Mark back on the team quickly it seems Paul, the sent-out one, was focused on the work while Barnabas, the encourager, was focused on the person. Don't miss how missionary teams are made up in the New Testament! Paul is called a sent-out one more than anyone else in the New Testament so we can feel confident one of his gifts was apostolic: gifted to go where the gospel was not and to form new churches. He was teamed with another sent-out one who was also strongly gifted as an encourager. Different gifts work together on the missionary team. Wanted: gifted encouragers to serve on missionary teams!

At the conclusion of the first journey, Paul wrote to three of the churches planted. The letter he wrote is the book of Galatians. In that letter, Paul called James, the half-brother of Jesus, a sent-out one, an apostle (Gal 1:19). James the half-brother of Jesus, like Barnabas, is not one of the twelve apostles. We know some things about James, like we did about Barnabas. James seems to be serving as the leading elder/pastor of the church at Jerusalem (Acts 15:31; 21;17) and churches were being planted

56

throughout Judea (Acts 9:31). We also know that James was connected to Jewish Christians scattered outside Judea (Jam 1:1). Since he is called an apostle, I wonder if James might have gone for a short time before he became the leading pastor at Jerusalem (maybe like a two-year "journeyman" term) and had been a part of planting the house churches to which these Christians belonged. James appears to have a primary gifting as a pastor/teacher and is called an apostle. Many missionary teams have been gifted with a team member who uses a gifting as a pastor/teacher to disciple new believers and to have a clear picture of how the church can be formed. Serving for a few years planting churches in unreached places can be wonderful background for someone who pastors a church for decades starting many churches in the surrounding areas. Wanted: pastor/teachers to serve on missionary teams!

Others are also called apostles, sent-out ones, in the New Testament who are not part of the twelve. This group of missionaries or sent-out ones could be those mentioned in 1 Cor 12:28-29, "And God has appointed in the church first apostles, second prophets, third teachers... Are all apostles? Are all prophets? Are all teachers...?" Ephesians 4:11 also makes sense with this understanding of apostles who are not part of the twelve. "And he gave the apostles, the prophets, the evangelists, the shepherds and teachers to equip the saints for the work of ministry, for building up the body of Christ" (Eph 4:11-12).

The connection of the terms apostle and missionary was noted by David Hesselgrave: "Both words carry the idea of one who is sent forth to do a task."[47] Concerning Paul's use of the word "apostles" in the list of spiritual gifts in 1 Corinthians, Craig Bloomberg explains, "Clearly, he is using the term in its root sense of those sent out on a mission, in this case a divinely commissioned one. Christians would later come to call such people missionaries or church-planters."[48] Don Dent, in his book, *The Ongoing Role of Apostles in Missions; The Forgotten Foundation,* explains: "apostles, now commonly called missionaries, are God's ongoing gift for the initial planting phase of the church among every people, to the end of the age."[49] Plainly, there are others who were included in the New Testament's use of the word "apostle," not as members of the twelve apostles, but matching the New Testament's description of sent-out ones.

ACTIVITY OF SENT-OUT ONES

After describing his desire to preach Christ where He was not known in Romans fifteen, Paul continues by mentioning his plans to go on to Spain. He states his reason for departing the regions of Asia minor, Macedonia, and Achaia: "Since I no longer have any room for work in these regions," or as the NLT states, "now I have finished my work in these regions." Obviously, there were still many lost in those regions. Obviously, there was still discipling that needed to take place. This passage clarifies what the sent-out task was in Paul's mind. Two verses earlier Paul had shared his ambition, his understanding of his work: "I make it my ambition to preach the gospel, not where Christ has already been named, so that I would not build on another man's foundation" (Rom 15:20-21). Going where the gospel was not known and leaving the first churches was Paul's work. Commenting on Paul's words in Rom 15:23, F. F. Bruce notes,

> The statement that he 'no longer has any room for work in these regions' throws light on Paul's conception of his task. There was certainly much room for further work in the area already evangelized by Paul, but not (as he conceived it) work of an apostolic nature. The work of an apostle was to preach the gospel where it had not been heard before and plant churches where none had existed before. When those churches had received sufficient teaching to enable them to understand their Christian status and responsibility, the apostle moved on to continue the same kind of work elsewhere.[50]

This explanation of Paul's thinking is consistent with the church planting described in Acts. This understanding is reflected by Eckhard Schnabel who writes, "Paul understands himself as pioneer missionary, called by God to 'plant' and to 'lay the foundation' (1 Cor 3:6, 10), that is, to establish new churches."[51] Since Paul is referred to as an apostle more than anyone else in the New Testament, he provides a good example of other things sent-out ones do in the body of Christ. Sent-out ones are sent to where the gospel is not (Rom 15:20-21), preach the gospel, gather the believers into a new church, and teach them, providing leaders, which is how Paul summarized his ministry in 1 Tim 2:7 and 2 Tim 1:11. Don Dent distinguishes between the twelve as laying the foundation for the universal church and missionary apostles: "The twelve apostles laid the foundation of the universal church; missionary apostles lay the foundation of the church in pioneer areas."[52] Paul further clarified that sent-out ones are concerned for the "care of all the churches" (2 Cor 11:28), genuinely concerned for all the churches planted. At its very heart, the task of "sent-out ones" in the New Testament has church planting as a necessary element.

The passage in Ephesians four clarifies another of the duties of sent-out ones. They are to equip the saints so that every believer can be ready to do what the nameless brothers did, scattered by persecution in Acts eight and eleven, ordinary believers planting churches wherever they go that needs a church. Sent-out ones equip the saints to make disciples of other ethnicities as they go through life. Sent-out ones help the church understand God's vision for the nations and how every believer can be a part of the gospel getting to every last place and person.

CHAPTER SIX: CLARIFYING THE COMMISSION

We have considered the works of God as described in the Old Testament and the things which Jesus began to do and teach as described in Luke which ends with a clarifying focus. God has prepared every believer to join him in his works, to be a part of his mission. However, all believers are never referred to as apostles in the New Testament and there is no single gift that every believer has. Considering that, a question comes to mind. Are those believers who are not gifted as apostles, not called to be missionaries, are they exempt from the gospel going to the ends of the earth? While the New Testament describes a gift of being an apostle and never includes all believers in that group, Jesus Christ unmistakably gave marching orders to all Christians that has them included in missions, in making disciples of all nations. Those marching orders are found in the Great Commission.

THE SETTING OF THE GREAT COMMISSION

Matthew begins the account of the Great Commission with a geographic location addressing the question of where—where were they? "Now the eleven disciples went to Galilee, to the mountain to which Jesus had directed them" (Matt 28:16). On the evening of his betrayal, the Lord's Supper was completed. Jesus and the eleven had gone to the Mount of Olives (Matt 26:30). Before Judas arrived with the soldiers, and before Jesus' prayer in the garden of Gethsemane, Jesus had instructed his disciples, "After I have been raised, I will go ahead of you to Galilee." Early Sunday morning on Resurrection Day, the angel had told the two

Mary's, "Then go quickly and tell his disciples that he has risen from the dead, and behold, he is going before you to Galilee; there you will see him" (Matt 28:7). On the afternoon of the resurrection Jesus had appeared to the two on the road to Emmaus and then they returned to Jerusalem (Luke 24:33). That evening the disciples were together behind closed doors when Jesus appeared to them, the account of which is found in Luke 24 and John 20:19-26 (including what has been called Luke's commission and John's commission).[53] A week later the group was again inside, this time with Thomas, and Jesus appeared again (John 20:26-29). These events all took place *in and around Jerusalem*. But Jesus and the angel had spoken *of Galilee*. In John 21, seven of the disciples were fishing at the Sea of Galilee, but Matthew 28 mentions at least eleven on a mountain. The location of the Great Commission doesn't match the other post resurrection appearances described in the gospels. The ascension scene in Acts one takes place on the Mount of Olives, just outside Jerusalem. While the details given rule out most of the other resurrection appearances mentioned in the New Testament, there is one account that could match.

In 1 Corinthians fifteen, Paul deals with the Corinthians' doubts about the resurrection. He begins by reminding them of the gospel which he preached. "Now I would remind you, brothers, of the gospel I preached ... that Christ died for our sins in accordance with the Scriptures, that he was buried, that he was raised on the third day in accordance with the Scriptures, and that he appeared to" witnesses (1 Cor. 15:1, 3-5a). As Paul lists the resurrection appearances, he mentions five or six of the ten accounts found in the Gospels and Acts one.[54] Paul highlights the importance of the appearance to the five hundred at one time by adding, "most of whom are still alive" (1 Cor 15:6), stressing that many of these could still verify that they personally saw the risen Lord, they were eyewitnesses. The appearances in Jerusalem or at the Sea of Tiberias don't match this event. Leon Morris suggests a connection to the Great

Commission, ""The appearance to *above five hundred brethren at once* may be that referred to in Mt. xxviii. 16ff. Otherwise it is mentioned here only. It is obviously of the first importance, for on no other occasion could such a large number of people testify to the fact of the resurrection."[55] A. T. Robertson stated it with certainty, "This incident is the one described in Mt 28:16 the prearranged meeting on the mountain in Galilee."[56] It seems likely that some record is given of the meeting with five hundred at one time. The possibility that the eleven were joined by such a large group answers another question that arises from the second verse of the paragraph containing the Great Commission.

Matthew continues his account of the Great Commission with some details of who was present. "And when they saw him they worshiped him, but some doubted" (Matt 28:17). The first part of the verse is easy to understand. They worshiped him! Remember, in the earlier appearance of the second Sunday, doubting Thomas [57] had so thoroughly had his questions answered that he cried out, "My Lord and my God!" (John 20:28). The eleven had watched Jesus eat fish, they had seen his hands and side. That same amazing joy, certainty, confidence, and faith mark the accounts of those who had already seen the resurrected Christ:

"They rose that same hour and returned to Jerusalem. And they found the eleven and those who were with them gathered, saying, *"The Lord has risen indeed, and has appeared to Simon!"* Then they told what had happened on the road, and how *he was known to them in the breaking of the bread*" (Luke 24:33-35, emphasis added).

"Mary Magdalene went and announced to the disciples, "I have seen the Lord"—and that he had said these things to her" (John 20:18);

"So the other disciples told [Thomas], 'We have seen the Lord,'" (John 20:25).

"None of the disciples dared ask him, 'Who are you?' They knew it was the Lord" (John 21:12).

It seems extremely unlikely that one of the eleven was still doubting. But if the five hundred were present, of course some of them could have doubted![58] Whether there were just eleven present for the giving of the Commission, or five hundred, it may be helpful to point out that the New Testament church made up of baptized believers indwelt by the Holy Spirit, did not yet exist.[59] The Great Commission was given to every individual believer! Of course, many churches faithfully dedicate themselves to the apostles teaching (Acts 2:42), through the words of the New Testament, and therefore make the proclamation to the nations of forgiveness in his name the focus to what they do (Luke 24:45-47). Every church making disciples, taught to obey all that he commanded, stresses the marching orders of the Savior. However, should believers find themself in a church that is not mentioning missions they can know that they are not excluded from God's focus for history. Every believer was included in Jesus' marching orders! While there is nothing in the text that would exempt every Christian to be included in Jesus' words *even if only* eleven were present, the scene is overwhelming if indeed Jesus gave these powerful words to the largest group who saw him alive after the cross! What a message for that great assembly!

BEGINNING THE COMMISSION

Jesus introduced the Great Commission with the clearest possible description of his authority to give the command he was about to make. And Jesus came and said to them, "All authority in heaven and on earth has been given to me" (Matt 28:18). The risen Lord had been given all authority and there is no limitation of his authority based on sphere. There is no place where he does not have authority. He has all authority here and there. He has all authority now and forever. As believers, the reminder is powerful. We made a commitment to follow him. We submitted to him as the Lord of our lives. Here, the rightness of that relationship is unmistakable. He has all authority. While many other voices may give us many other instructions, the sweet voice of our Savior, the one who has all authority, gives this one.

The one who has the right to give a command commanded all believers, "Go therefore and make disciples of all nations, baptizing them in the name of the Father and of the Son and of the Holy Spirit, teaching them to observe all that I have commanded you. And behold, I am with you always, to the end of the age" (Matt 28:19-20). Jesus began with a participle translated "Go therefore." When this participle is followed by an imperative, like it is here, the English translations treat it as an imperative.[60] However, the fact remains, it is not a command in the Greek but a participle. Herschel Hobbs states clearly, "'Go.' This is a participle, not an imperative. Literally, 'going' or 'as you go.' 'Teach.' This is the only imperative in the Commission. It means 'make disciples' or 'disciple'"[61] Rick Warren takes the same position as Hobbs, "The word *go* in the Great Commission is a participle in the Greek text. It should read 'as you are going.' It is every Christian's responsibility to share the Good News wherever we go."[62] Some have suggested that no disciples can be made without going across the street, going to where someone else is. Go is required but doesn't necessarily mean every believer is commanded to go across the globe. Craig Blomberg keeps the balance, "To 'make disciples of all nations' does require many people to leave their homelands, but Jesus' main focus remains on the task of all believers to duplicate themselves wherever they may be."[63] Either, leave family and job and go make disciples, or else, as you are going through your life make disciples. The command, "make disciples," is for everyone. As we discussed earlier, if your primary gifting is as a sent-out one or a missionary, or if you have sensed the Spirit's clear guidance that his will is for you to take a missionary assignment at this time, then you must leave and go. If not, then you are commanded to make disciples as you go through life. Two individuals in Acts provide examples of each of the possible interpretations of "go" in the Great Commission.

PHILIP – AN EXAMPLE OF "AS YOU GO"

Philip is never called an apostle or sent-out one. The story of Acts intersects with his story when the seven are named in Acts six to serve the body, most likely the first deacons.[64] When the religious persecution arose connected with the martyrdom of his fellow deacon, Stephen, Philip is among those that were scattered by the persecution. Philip probably would be called a refugee today, driven from his homeland by violence.

In response to the persecution in Jerusalem, Philip went to Samaria where he heralded the gospel of Jesus. We are later told (Acts 21:8-9) that Philip was an evangelist and what happens in Samaria makes this clear. The Holy Spirit validated his preaching in this new city with healings and demons being cast out. Many men and women believed the gospel as Philip preached it and they were baptized. When the apostles in Jerusalem heard of what God was doing, they sent Peter and John who testified, taught the word of God, and preached the gospel there and in surrounding villages. The next chapter reports churches in Samaria, for the first time in Acts (Acts 9:31).

While in the middle of the revival, "an angel of the Lord said to Philip, 'Rise and go toward the south to the road that goes down from Jerusalem to Gaza.' This is a desert place" (Acts 8:26). Philip immediately left the revival and went to the desert… where there just happened to be a caravan, with an Ethiopian eunuch, who was treasurer for the queen! He was reading Isaiah fifty-three. The Holy Spirit told Philip to join his chariot. Philip asked some questions and shared the gospel. The eunuch was saved and baptized. The chapter ends, "And when they came up out of the water, the Spirit of the Lord carried Philip away,[65] and the eunuch saw him no more, and went on his way rejoicing. But Philip found himself at Azotus, and as he passed through, he preached the gospel to all the towns until he came to Caesarea" (Acts 8:39-40). Jerusalem, Samaria, the desert road, now Caesarea Philippi.

The next time Philip is found in the book of Acts, twenty years have passed. He is still in Caesarea, raising his four daughters. When Paul and the missionary team come through town they connect with Philip, and he blesses them with hospitability. That's all we know! I find Philip to be an amazing example of how someone who was gifted as a servant and evangelist found himself scattered to the nations, kind of like on a short-term assignment or role. He used his gifts where he was as part of a larger church-planting team. And then, he continued to support missionaries as he had opportunity, but did not keep going to new places like a sent-out one.

I can picture this as a very faithful servant in a church today as a deacon or the lady who is always helping others, or maybe a very gifted evangelist who shares at work with the other nurses she works with, or who always shares the gospel in every home he goes to as a plumber. Phil, or Felipa, is always lifting up specific missionaries' requests, gives generously to missions' offerings, and has gone with the church on several mission trips. These believers are particularly excited when they get to share the gospel with someone from another ethnicity because the Great Commission is giant in their minds. Maybe Felipa served for two years overseas after college and is pouring a passion for the nations into her four daughters. They are in the very center of God's will, participating in his mission with eternity in focus, following the Spirit's lead.

PAUL – AN EXAMPLE OF COMMANDED TO GO

At the time of his conversion, Saul of Tarsus found out that his place in the body of Christ was as a sent-out one.[66] Paul is such a central figure in the second half of Acts that Luke records his conversion and then relates two accounts of Paul giving his testimony about his conversion. We learn different things each time.

In Acts twenty-six, Paul reveals that on the day he was saved, Jesus said, "I am Jesus whom you are persecuting. But rise and stand upon your feet, for I have appeared to you for this purpose, to appoint you as a servant and witness to the things in which you have seen me and to those in which I will appear to you, delivering you from your people and from *the Gentiles—to whom I am sending you* to open their eyes, so that they may turn from darkness to light and from the power of Satan to God, that they may receive forgiveness of sins and a place among those who are sanctified by faith in me" (Acts 26:15-18, emphasis added). Jesus told him on the road to Damascus that he was sending Paul as an apostle to the Gentiles. Jesus also gave him that day many of the key points that would shape his theology until the day he died: salvation is by faith in Jesus, salvation includes forgiveness of sins and sanctification, that the Gentiles who are saved have a place in the body of Christ with Jews, that the lost are held in the power of Satan and darkness, and may receive forgiveness of sins turning to light and God.

It was very important to Paul that he was not sent-out by any human group but by God. When he wrote the churches of Galatia, he described it like this: "Paul, an apostle (not sent from men nor through the agency of man, but through Jesus Christ and God the Father, who raised Him from the dead)"[67] (Gal 1:1 NASB), or as the NLT words it, "This letter is from Paul, an apostle. I was not appointed by any group of people or any human authority, but by Jesus Christ himself and by God the Father, who raised Jesus from the dead." Paul followed the Holy Spirit's leadership to go where the gospel was not, evangelize, make disciples, form them into a church with leaders, and then go to another place, often with new teammates from the last place.[68]

Paul was not content that the gospel would get to a new place. He was not content supporting others that went or praying for them as they went. His understanding of the gifts and role, the marching orders that he had received from the Lord that day on the road to Damascus meant that *he was compelled to go personally*. Listen to his words from Romans 15. "I make it my ambition to preach the gospel, not where Christ has already been named, lest I build on someone else's foundation, but as it is written, 'Those who have never been told of him will see, and those who have never heard will understand'" (Rom 15:20-21). This is the heartbeat of a sent-out one. Those who are missionaries hear a divine "go" and it means leave home and family to go where he sends. Paul and Philip provide two examples of how the "go" of the Great Commission was applied in Acts.

THE IMPERATIVE OF THE GREAT COMMISSION

After the introductory participle "Go" or "As you are going," Jesus gave the command of the Great Commission: "make disciples." It is interesting that none of the passages referred to as commissions in Luke twenty-four, John twenty, and Acts one have an imperative in the verses. Noting a similar theme in the closing words of Luke twenty-four and Acts 1:8, David Bosch points out, "Luke presents all this, not in the form of a mandate or commission, as Matthew does, but rather in the form of a fact and a promise."[69] So it is safe to say that the only imperative in any of the New Testament "commissions" is to make disciples.[70] The wording of the command is very interesting. Jesus did not say to try to make disciples. He did not say to work at it. He gave a very clear command that has only one way to obey it: make a disciple. The two participles that follow the command give information about how to make those disciples.

Baptizing them implies preaching the gospel to which they respond with repentance and faith, since responding to the gospel with repentance and faith is what precede baptism in the New Testament. Baptism would then make them part of the fellowship of a local church.[71]

Next Jesus explained that his command to make disciples required "teaching them to obey everything I have commanded you" (NIV). The word translated "observe" or "obey" is often translated "keep," making clear this is not *thinking* about obedience but requires doing what Jesus said, or obedience. In John 14:15, the night before the cross, Jesus said, "If you love me, you will *keep* my commandments." Connecting love for God with keeping his commandments went all the way back to Deuteronomy 11:22-23, "For *if* you are careful to *keep* all this *commandment* which I am commanding you to do, to *love the LORD your God*, to walk in all His ways and hold fast to Him, then the LORD will drive out all these nations from before you, and you will dispossess nations greater and mightier than you" (NASB, emphasis added). 1 John 2:4 uses the same word, "Whoever says 'I know him' but does not *keep* his commandments is a liar, and the truth is not in him," making clear that the word does not mean just knowing the commandments but requires keeping or obeying his commands. In order to have disciples that keep his commandments, it is necessary to teach them what he commanded or else to teach them how to know his commands from Scripture. But knowledge is not enough. The disciples being made must be taught to keep, observe, or obey.

Interestingly, one of the commands that would have to be taught to new disciples would certainly be this command, the Great Commission. If I make a disciple that has been taught to keep his commands (including the Great Commission), then the second generation would have to make a disciple that will keep his commands (including the Great Commission), and then third generation would have to make a disciple that will keep his commands (including the Great Commission), and then the fourth.... Jesus' wording is amazing. This simple, well-known command produces multiplication of disciples anywhere it is followed.[72] The wording is so precise that we can recognize that anywhere the multiplication of disciples has stopped, the generation of believers before that moment must have stopped obeying the commission.

THE POWER TO OBEY THE GREAT COMMISSION

This idea of making disciples that make disciples that make disciples sounds pretty impossible for human beings. And, actually, it is. But Jesus said he would be with us always. His presence provides all that is needed to obey his commands. As Paul famously said, "I can do all things through him who strengthens me" (Phil 4:13). All things would certainly include Jesus' marching orders for believers. The specific focus in 2 Corinthians nine is monetary giving, but the words talk about having "sufficiency in all things" to "abound in every good work," certainly more inclusive words than just an offering. Paul wrote, "The point is this: whoever sows sparingly will also reap sparingly, and whoever sows bountifully will also reap bountifully... And *God is able to make all grace abound* to you, so that having all *sufficiency in all things* at all times, *you may abound in every good work*" (2 Cor 9:6, 8, emphasis added). God always empowers us to obey the commands he gives us (Heb 13:21; Phil 2:13; Isa 26:12). The ability to obey the Great Commission is beyond us. I can't. But, not to worry, he can.

So, every Christian is to make disciples either going or as they go, disciples that are baptized, or incorporated into the fellowship of a church, and are taught to keep, observe, or obey Christ's commands. One last detail. Every believer is assumed to share with his family and friends about the forgiveness of sin, abundant life, and freedom from an eternity without Christ. That is only natural. According to Jesus' description, even the lost want their *family members* to hear the gospel and avoid a Christless eternity once they clearly understand eternal realities![73] It is natural to

71

want to share such important good news with those you love. What is not natural, is to reach out to other ethnicities, other groups, to those who are not in my circle. But if every believer looks for opportunities to make a disciple of another ethnicity, or group, then the gospel jumps to another segment and begins spreading naturally throughout that segment. Then some from that segment will come into contact with another ethnicity or group and the gospel will spread to that group. The commission makes all believers look for other ethnicities or groups in which they can make a disciple. And when they do, the gospel spreads rapidly, as Paul prayed in 2 Thess 3:1. "Finally, brothers, pray for us, that the word of the Lord may speed ahead and be honored, as happened among you."

CHAPTER SEVEN: THE SENT-OUT TASK IN SCRIPTURE

Involvement in any part of the broad mission of God can be appropriate for believers as long as they join God in his work while maintaining a focus on eternity (particularly the historical highlights of Christ's coming to pay for sin and the need for that message to be preached to all) and they are following the Spirit's leadership. Some are called to become more directly involved in the work of missions, either by gifting and calling (which would lead to a long-term focus on missions), or by assignment or role (which could be a sense that God has guided to accept this two-year missions' assignment or life's events putting you in a missions' setting). The Great Commission is for all believers as they go through life. However, for a window of time or for a focus of their lives, some are to leave family, profession, and home (Matt 4:18-22); to be involved in the sent-out task. What specifically is meant in Scripture by the sent-out task? The first missionary journey began when "the Holy Spirit said, 'Set apart for me Barnabas and Saul for *the work* to which I have called them'" (Acts 13:2, emphasis added). As the first journey ended the team returned "to Antioch, where they had been commended to the grace of God for *the work* that they had fulfilled" (Acts 14:26, emphasis added). What was the work, the missionary task, as described in the New Testament?[74] Many outlines have been suggested, sometimes just different ways of stating the same process, the process described in Scripture. The International Mission Board currently speaks of six component parts of the missionary task: entry, evangelism, discipleship, church formation, leadership development, and exit to a new field. These elements can be seen over and over again in the book of Acts, but Paul's work at Corinth provides an easy place to describe the sent-out-task in Scripture.

ENTRY

Acts 18:1-6

[1]After this Paul left Athens and went to Corinth. [2]And he found a Jew named Aquila, a native of Pontus, recently come from Italy with his wife Priscilla, because Claudius had commanded all the Jews to leave Rome. And he went to see them, [3]and because he was of the same trade he stayed with them and worked, for they were tentmakers by trade. [4]And he reasoned in the synagogue every Sabbath, and tried to persuade Jews and Greeks.

[5]When Silas and Timothy arrived from Macedonia, Paul was occupied with the word, testifying to the Jews that the Christ was Jesus. [6]And when they opposed and reviled him, he shook out his garments and said to them, "Your blood be on your own heads! I am innocent. From now on I will go to the Gentiles."

The second missionary journey provides an excellent study in entry. As Paul and Silas left Antioch, they went back to the churches planted during the first journey. Timothy, who appears to have been one of the converts on the first journey, joined the team at Lystra (Acts 15:41-16:5). Paul intended to go to Asia minor, probably to Ephesus. The doors were closed, although they eventually did go to Ephesus on the third journey. God's "no" was more like a "not now." The team went to Philippi (a leading city of the district, Acts 16:12) where they started a group "down by the riverside." They found Lydia who was ready at that time to receive the gospel.[75] She opened her home, and it appears that a house church was planted there. Paul, being annoyed, cast a demon out of a slave girl (Acts 16:16-18), which resulted in his being beaten and thrown in prison (Acts 16:19-24). After forming another group in the jailer's home, Paul left Philippi. The church he had planted soon sent him financial support while he was in Thessalonica and again in Corinth, (the arrival of the support being described in 1 Cor 18:5).[76]

After his departure from Philippi, Paul entered Thessalonica going to the synagogue, as was his custom (Acts 17:2), the place where people had been exposed to the reading of Scripture.[77] Although Scripture only tells of three Sabbaths spent in Thessalonica, an exemplary church was planted.[78] Paul went from Thessalonica to the Bereans who carefully studied the Scriptures and to Athens where many believed, but the New Testament does not tell us of a church in either place, perhaps due to how quickly Paul was run out of each city.

Paul then *enters* Corinth. Having arrived at Corinth after being beaten with rods and imprisoned at Philippi, and then run out of Thessalonica, Berea and Athens, it is no surprise that Paul later said about his entry at Corinth, "And I was with you in weakness and in fear and much trembling (1 Cor 2:3). Paul's humanity is very apparent. He was afraid and was trembling. No need to sugar coat his words. That's what he said. Notwithstanding, he did go on to Corinth. This reminds us of the first journey. After being stoned to the point they thought he was dead at Lystra, Paul returned to the churches "strengthening the souls of the disciples, encouraging them to continue in the faith, and saying that through many tribulations we must enter the kingdom of God" (Acts 14:22). There is something about persevering in tribulations that lends credibility when you teach on persevering. Entry may mean that you have come through such chaos that you, afraid and trembling, are determined to "know nothing among you except Jesus Christ and him crucified" (1 Cor 2:2).

Such a challenging entry is not promised in every situation in Scripture, but don't be discouraged when it is.

As Paul entered Corinth, we are told that he found a couple named Aquila and Priscilla who had recently fled Rome because of persecution against the Jews. They appear not to be "down and out" but "up and out" because it seems they can move to new cities as they want and are able to establish businesses wherever they go.[79] In Corinth, they had established a tentmaking business and Paul joined them because he was of the same trade. This passage provides another insight about entry.

Sometimes tentmaking is necessary to be in a city. By tentmaking I am referring to a secondary reason to be in the city for the primary purpose of the missionary task. For Paul, the secondary reason actually involved making real tents. Here, the reason appears to be financial. Initially Paul seems to be making tents five or six days a week and then on the Sabbath he is trying "to persuade Jews and Greeks" (Acts 18:4). However, as soon as Silas and Timothy arrived from Macedonia with the offering, Paul began occupying himself completely with the word (Acts 18:6; Phil 4:15-16). So, if the reason for having a secondary reason to be in a city (tentmaking) is financial, it is good to limit the time invested in that secondary endeavor and stop it completely when possible. There are other reasons for tentmaking.

In 1 Samuel sixteen we read of a fascinating time when the Lord told Samuel to go anoint a new king in Bethlehem. Samuel points out that the current king, Saul, might hear about it and kill Samuel. Yahweh then says, "Take a heifer with you and say, 'I have come to sacrifice to the LORD.' And invite Jesse to the sacrifice, and I will show you what you shall do. And you shall anoint for me him whom I declare to you" (1 Sam 16:2-3). The Lord himself provided Samuel with a secondary, legitimate reason to be in the city so that he could complete his primary assignment. We must be very careful not to suggest it is wrong to say we are there for one purpose and then, in addition to doing what we said, to complete the Lord's business. The text is explicit that this was the Lord's idea. However, if the reason we are tentmaking is to have a legitimate reason to be in a city or country, integrity demands that we do what we said we would do and we keep doing it as long as we said. Entry sometimes includes finding a way to be legally or legitimately present in a certain place.

Another thought needs to be added regarding the gift received from the Macedonians, the Philippians in particular. Paul allowed others to partner with him in the work. He later described their sending this gift as partnership. "And you Philippians yourselves know that in the beginning of the gospel, when I left Macedonia, no church entered into partnership with me in giving and receiving, except you only" (Phil 4:15). Since the text says Philippi was *the only church* that did this, Antioch did not. No church from the first journey did. The recently planted, new, impoverished church at Philippi did! Later Paul would write to this church at Corinth and use the example of the giving to another offering of these same churches in Macedonia to motivate the Corinthians. "We want you to know, brothers, about the grace of God that has been given among the churches of Macedonia, for in a severe test of affliction, their abundance of joy and their extreme poverty have overflowed in a wealth of generosity on their part" (2 Cor 8:1-2). So, in entry Paul did not bring money to give out. He never did. Money is often mentioned in church planting in the New Testament.[80] However, it never flows toward a new church. Money always flows away from the new churches, even when those new churches are very poor. Giving strengthens believers because God provides the grace to give. Giving away rice or money to start a new church often produces "rice Christians," or at least opens the door to that accusation. Dependency on money is never a problem in church planting when the church planter follows the New Testament practices of only receiving money *from* the church plants.

The New Testament pictures the new churches planted as a source of giving and blessing. When missionaries plant a church, they have planted a fountain of ministry in that new place, a well-spring for all the mission of God in that community. The church plant in Antioch provides a specific example of a new church meeting the needs of the poor.

> The offering collected in the new church in Antioch was to minister to the needs of the poor—believers in new churches are to demonstrate the love of Christ. Jesus had compassion for the sick (see Matt. 14:14; 20:34), the hungry (see 15:32), those mourning the death of loved ones (see Luke 7:12–13), and those who were "distressed and dispirited" (Matt. 9:36). When we consider the direction of the money flow above, the pattern seems to be that sent-out ones focus on evangelism, discipleship, and church planting, leaving a local body of believers that then ministers to the poor and needy. Of course, the sent-out ones are to model the Christian life (including ministry to the poor), because they are first followers of Christ and then sent-out ones.[81]

In the book of Acts, ministry to the poor is more a result of church planting than a part of planting a church. Long-term ministry was never described as part of how a church was planted in Acts. The churches planted ministered in beautiful ways! New churches are an amazing out-post of all that the body of Christ does.

EVANGELISM

Acts 16:4-8

[4]And he reasoned in the synagogue every Sabbath, and tried to persuade Jews and Greeks.[5]When Silas and Timothy arrived from Macedonia, Paul was occupied with the word, testifying to the Jews that the Christ was Jesus. [6]And when they opposed and reviled him, he shook out his garments and said to them, "Your blood be on your own heads! I am innocent. From now on I will go to the Gentiles." [7]And he left there and went to the house of a man named Titius Justus, a worshiper of God. His house was next door to the synagogue. [8]Crispus, the ruler of the

synagogue, believed in the Lord, together with his entire household. And many of the Corinthians hearing Paul believed and were baptized.

Paul began in Corinth going to the synagogue trying, "to persuade Jews and Greeks." The evangelism style employed in the early days of Corinth is described as persuasion which brings to mind apologetics and giving a reason for the hope that is within (1 Pet 3:15). We have already seen that Paul later described his approach as avoiding lofty speech or wisdom but instead focusing solely on Jesus as the Christ who was crucified (2 Cor 2:1-2). The emphasis sounds strangely like Jesus' words in Luke twenty-four about the Messiah's death which should be proclaimed to the nations!

Following the arrival of Silas and Timothy with the financial gift from Philippi, Paul was, "occupied with the word, testifying to the Jews that the Christ was Jesus" (Acts 18:5). His response when they opposed and reviled him makes a clear textual connection to the person of peace model. When Acts 18:6 says, "he shook out his garments," the English text is translating a verb (*ektinassō*, ἐκτινάσσω) which has been used three previous times in the New Testament. In Matthew ten and Mark six the verb is used in the person of peace instructions that Jesus gave to the twelve as he sent them out. The third use is found in Acts 13:51, on the first journey when Paul left those who resisted the gospel message. In the first journey Paul was working in villages so he went to the next village. Here in Corinth, Paul was working in a major city, so he did not leave the city, but went next door to another people group. After leaving the synagogue and going to the Jews something fascinating happens. "And he left there and went to the house of a man named Titius Justus, a worshiper of God. His house was next door to the synagogue. Crispus, *the ruler of the synagogue, believed* in the Lord, together with his entire household" (Acts 18:7-8, emphasis added). When Paul left and went to another group, the person who was saved was Crispus, the ruler of the synagogue! This passage provides several ideas about the person of peace model. The person of peace model is based on the idea that the missionary is not bringing God to a new place, but that God has always been there and has been at work. Specifically, the sent-out one enters the new place believing that God has been working and looking for a way to join God in his works (John 5:19). The sent-out one believes that God is drawing some to himself at that very time (John 16:6-8 and 12:32-33). If the sent-out ones enter a resistant household, they believe they are not at the correct starting place because God has prepared some already and they want to join the work of God. Paul does not shake the dust off because he does not care for Crispus. The sent-out ones believe God is an all-wise Lord of the Harvest and the best thing they can do for anyone on the planet is to obey him. When the sent-out ones encounter the prepared person or household, the less interested people notice the transformation that came from receiving the Spirit and being born again. It is like the less interested people could say, "I don't know those strangers who came to town. They don't speak the language very well. And they don't seem to like to get drunk like we do. But ol' Cris, he used to be just like us. He beat his wife just like we do. He cheated just like we do. And now, look at him! Something has happened to ol' Cris. He is a new man. Whatever happened to him is powerful. I need that. I don't know these strangers, but I want what happened to ol' Cris!" The transformed lives of those prepared by God can lead the less receptive to then follow Christ! The person of peace model is often used in Entry and in Evangelism.

Even with the response of Crispus who believed together with his entire household, and the many Corinthians who were believing and being baptized, Paul was still afraid. The verb tense used in verse nine implies he was to stop an action that was already ongoing. The great apostle Paul was afraid. In a strange way, that is surprisingly encouraging. If God can use Paul when he is afraid, then he can use me. Be careful not to make much of Paul. *Make much of Paul's God who also lives in you!* God has only used one perfect person in all human history, that would be Jesus. Outside of him, God is used to using people like us! Yes, God can use people who get afraid, but don't miss what God says to them: Stop it! Hundreds of times in Scripture we are told not to be afraid, because God is with us! That is precisely what Paul is told. "Stop being afraid because I am with you." Paul had a lone-ranger complex, much like Elijah, who had said, "I alone am left" (1 Kings 19:10, 14), when he had been told of one hundred fellow servants (1 Kings 18:13). Actually, there were seven thousand others who had not bowed the knee (1 Kings 19:18). Paul was feeling all alone *even though "many... believed"* (18:8) so the Lord reminded him he already had "many in this city who are my people."[82] Paul appears to have followed the Lord's instructions and dealt with his fear because he stayed another eighteen months in the city.

DISCIPLESHIP

Following the Lord's encouraging words, Paul settled down for his longest period of ministry up to this point.[83] For a year and six months, he taught the word of God among them. The balanced perspective of the New Testament concerning discipleship in church planting is amazing. Discipleship is emphasized in every church plant in Acts. Even though Paul often had to leave quickly in the church plants before Corinth, he wrote back to the churches of the first journey, as well as Philippi and Thessalonica of the second journey, continuing their discipleship. He returned to each church plant in Acts on subsequent visits and mentored leaders by having them travel with him. Paul and Barnabas stayed one year at Antioch (Acts 11:26). Paul stayed a year-and-a-half at Corinth (Acts 18:11) and taught for two years at the school of Tyrannus in Ephesus (Acts 19:9-10), for a total of three years there (Acts 20:31). During that time the gospel went throughout the region, "so that all who lived in Asia heard the word of the Lord" (Acts 19:10). In the epistles, Paul refers to the things he taught them while present (2 Thess 2:5) and it is amazing! Paul practiced sound discipleship! But don't miss, he never stayed ten years. He never stayed five. He only stayed longer than eighteen months one time (and on that occasion the gospel spread through the region). Acts clearly pictures sound discipleship, but also pictures sent-out ones trusting the Holy Spirit, in the new believers, to be the real teacher (Acts 14:23; 20:32; 1 John 2:27). Sent-out ones remember why they were sent, like Jesus before them: "the crowds were searching for Him, and came to Him and tried to keep Him from going away from them. But He said to them, 'I must preach the kingdom of God to *the other cities also*, for I was sent (apostled, sent out) for this purpose'" (Luke 4:42-43, emphasis added).

The church plant in Corinth also provides us a beautiful example of how discipleship worked in the New Testament. As we saw in the Great Commission, disciples made disciples who made disciples. Paul clearly states this principle in 2 Tim 2:2. "and what you have heard from me in the presence of many witnesses entrust to faithful men, who will be able to teach others also." Paul taught Timothy, Timothy taught faithful men, faithful men taught others also: disciples making disciples to the fourth generation. When Paul arrived at Corinth, Aquila and Priscilla were probably not believers.[84] But they spent eighteen months with Paul and appear to have come to faith and been discipled. They then went with him to Ephesus where they discipled a promising, gifted brother named Apollos (Acts 18:24-26). Apollos then wanted to go back to Corinth (Acts 18:27-28) and discipled many (1 Cor 3:6). Disciples made disciples to the fourth generation.

CHURCH FORMATION

When Paul wrote back to the Corinthians from Ephesus (Acts 19:10), he spoke of them as "the church of God that is in Corinth, to those sanctified in Christ Jesus, called to be saints together with all those who in every place call upon the name of our Lord Jesus Christ, both their Lord and ours" (1 Cor 2:1). They were a messy church. They had serious divisions (1 Cor 1-3), gross immorality (1 Cor 5), lawsuits against each other (1 Cor 6), problems with the Lord's supper (1 Cor 11), confusion about spiritual gifts (1 Cor 12-14), and they even questioned the resurrection (1 Cor 15). Not every new church was exemplary like the Thessalonians! However, they were saints in Christ (1 Cor 1:2). They had the Holy Spirit who had placed them in the universal church (1 Cor 12:13). Paul could affirm to them, "in every way you were enriched in him in all speech and all knowledge" (1 Cor 1:5), "that you are not lacking in any gift" (1 Cor 1:7) and that the Lord Jesus would "sustain you to the end, guiltless in the day of our Lord Jesus Christ" (1 Cor 1:8).

Paul spent eighteen months forming them into a church. Apollos pastored them. Paul wrote them twice from Ephesus (1 Cor 5:9 and 1:1). He came back to visit them for three months at the end of the third journey (Acts 20:2-3). And then he wrote 2 Corinthians to continue their discipleship and church formation.

No one aims at planting a messy church, but it even happened to Paul! Furthermore, the Holy Spirit meant for us to know about it! Paul models personal investment, using technology at hand, and continuing until "Christ is formed in you" as Paul said to the Galatians (4:19) or until they "all attain to the unity of the faith and of the knowledge of the Son of God, to mature manhood, to the measure of the stature of the fullness of Christ, so that we may no longer be children, tossed to and fro by the waves and carried about by every wind of doctrine, by human cunning, by craftiness in deceitful schemes. Rather, speaking the truth in love, we are to grow up in every way into him who is the head, into Christ," as Paul said to the Ephesians (4:13-15).

LEADERSHIP DEVELOPMENT

The story of Aquila and Priscilla is a beautiful picture of leadership development. By Paul's mentoring them and spending time with them during the eighteen months in Corinth, Aquila and Priscilla were so thoroughly trained as leaders that they were able to replicate the leadership development they had received in the life of Apollos.

They are also an amazing example of leadership development because they had watched Paul start the church in Corinth. They then went and planted a church in their home in Ephesus: "The churches of Asia send you greetings. Aquila and Prisca, together with the church in their house, send you hearty greetings in the Lord" (1 Cor 16:19). They subsequently moved back to Rome and planted another church in their house: "Greet Prisca and Aquila, my fellow workers in Christ Jesus, who risked their necks for my life, to whom not only I give thanks but all the churches of the Gentiles give thanks as well. Greet also the church in their house" Rom 16:3-5). Notice the respect given in Scripture to those who have risked their necks for the gospel, and that is the kind of leaders that Paul developed!

EXIT TO A NEW FIELD

Corinth provides the perfect example of exiting to the next field. When Paul left Corinth, Aquila and Priscilla accompanied him to Ephesus, the next field. They were such a part of the team, that they had one of the house churches in Ephesus meeting in their home. Paul had modeled exiting so well that when they mentored Apollos as a leader, they also helped him go to another place, back to Corinth. While Aquila and Priscilla are not called apostles in the New Testament, they certainly look like missionaries because they do not just plant a church in their city when there is not one (like the unnamed brothers in Antioch), but they keep going to new places. Paul is carefully going to the next city, and he instilled this passion in others. For Paul in Corinth, leaving certainly did not mean forsaking. As was noted, he continued to visit, continued to write, continued to invest in this church long after he left.

Entry, evangelism, discipleship, church formation, leadership development and exit to a new field, the component parts of the missionary task are seen in Corinth. This is what sent-out ones did in the New Testament. This is what sent-out ones do today.

CONCLUSION

The questions of the new workers were sometimes verbalized and sometimes just visible on their faces. As they heard biblical explanations of the missionary task, the focus left out so many things that they had always associated with being on mission, with being missional, with being missionary. During the session on the missionary task, where were the presentations on ministering to the poor and the suffering? Climate? Trafficking? Social Justice? Where are all the passages on meeting human needs in the book of Acts' descriptions of the missionary task? Scriptures' answer to the questions can be connected to two important ideas mentioned in the first two verses of the introduction to Acts. Scripture provides guidance for placing missionaries in the mission of God.

Luke had first written one of the gospels describing the three decades of Jesus' life on earth. He was introducing the second half of his history that was going to describe the expansion of the kingdom for the next three decades: from the ascension of Jesus Christ to Paul's arrival and ministry in Rome. The introduction bridging those two periods contains two phrases that masterfully connect the two works. In Acts 1:1 Luke summarizes his gospel as describing "all that Jesus began to do and teach." In Acts 2:2 he mentions "the apostles whom he had chosen." The first phrase provided us a starting place to discuss the works of God, mission of God, the first half of this two-volume history. The second phrase provided us a starting place to place missionaries in the mission of God, the second half of this work.

Jesus did not stop doing and teaching all that he "began to do and teach" in the Gospel of Luke. He began to do and teach those things while walking on earth. He continued to do those things throughout the book of Acts. Today, he is still doing and teaching the things he did and taught in Luke, through his body, the church. As we walked through the chapters of Luke's gospel, in chapter one, we were struck by the breadth of "all that Jesus began to do and teach." He was moved by compassion and acted to meet people's needs. As he was making disciples, he taught how to live the victorious, Christian life. He taught the disciples to look for his return, while faithfully serving during the delay. He repeatedly foretold his death and resurrection. And then he died and rose again. Across the centuries and in every corner of the globe, as Jesus lives the Christ-life through believers, he has continued to feed the hungry, to minister to the needy, to teach believers to live victoriously.

The things which "Jesus began to do and teach" are called the "works of God," a phrase which provided us a way to consider the breadth of what God the Father is doing from the perspective of the Old Testament, in chapter two. The works of God include his creation and ongoing care of the planet providing water and food for the animals and human beings. God is at work for justice in our world, particularly for the fatherless and widows. God's work includes forming every new human being. God's work includes showing mercy. The works of God, encompassing all he does, have been described as the mission of God. Working in a manner consistent with the mission of God could be called being missional. However, the breadth of what "Jesus began to do and teach" and the "works of God" was specifically, precisely focused when Jesus opened the disciples' minds to understand the Scriptures.

Jesus said that the focus of Scripture, the key to understanding Scripture, the overarching story of Scripture is about *the Messiah* ("Thus it is written, that the Christ should suffer and on the third day rise from the dead," Luke 24:46) *and the missionary task* ("and that repentance for the forgiveness of sins should be proclaimed in his name to all nations," Luke

24:47). In chapter three we traced the problem of sin and the need for a sacrifice all through the Old Testament. We traced, from Genesis to Malachi, God's desire for all nations and his desire that repentance for the forgiveness of sins should be proclaimed to all nations. However, the same focus, the Messiah and the missionary task, is also the outline of the New Testament, of all human history. The wise person who desires to live missionally, to live lined up with the mission of God, will join God in any of his works while always remembering that repentance and faith in Jesus' death and resurrection is the only way any person will be in heaven, and always remembering that God wants everyone to hear that good news.

While every believer who participates in any part of what "Jesus began to do and teach" or the "works of God" with the focus of the Messiah and the missionary task is living missionally, in chapter four we explored how God's gifting, commands, and opportunities guide believers how to be involved in the mission of God. Gifts are God's supernatural preparation for every believer to join in what he is doing. There is no gift that every believer has. However, God's commands apply to all believers. Therefore, every believer is commanded to serve but not all are gifted in service. Every believer is commanded to teach but not all are gifted teachers. Every believer is to make disciples of other ethnicities and groups, but not all are gifted or called as missionaries. Every believer is to encourage one another but not all have the gift of encouragement. Gifts provide an insight into how any believer is to fit into the mission of God, but they never exempt any believer from obeying God's commands. Gifts also do not exempt any Christian from following the Lord's guidance for a particular assignment or task. While walking in the Spirit, every believer is to live consistent with the mission of God maintaining a focus on the centrality of Christ's death and resurrection for salvation and God's passion that forgiveness of sins in his name be proclaimed to all nations. Chapters one through four brought us thus far. However, what about the missionary task? How does it fit into the mission of God?

In chapter five we looked carefully at two different ways the New Testament talks about apostles. The twelve apostles are such a closed group that they are named four times and still number twelve in eternity future. However, the second half the book of Acts focuses on those who are not named in the lists of the twelve. The New Testament unmistakably names Barnabas and others as sent-out ones, who provide examples of what missionaries do today.

Jesus' command in the Great Commission clearly applies to every believer even though in the New Testament all believers are not gifted as apostles or called missionaries, as we explored in chapter six. Those believers who are called and gifted as missionaries are to go, leaving family and country, to make disciples of the nations as a major ministry of their lives. All other believers are to make disciples of all nations as they go through life. Obedience to the Great Commission is central in their lives as they obey God's guidance to go as he leads, to support with prayer and giving. Of course, every believer is to obey should the Holy Spirit guide them to accept, for a period of time, a role or assignment in the missionary task. Such kingdom focus leads to multiplication of believers everywhere the Great Commission is obeyed. Every believer has a part in the missionary task.

The missionary task was the focus of chapter seven. While many different outlines can be used to describe the missionary task, one current way is to note entry, evangelism, discipleship, church formation, leadership development, and exit to a new field. Acts eighteen provides one place to clearly understand each component part of the missionary task. This is what the New Testament pictures as missions, as missionary, as the missionary task. This is how missionaries fit in the mission of God.

The focus of Scripture and history is on the Messiah and the missionary task. All Christians, while wisely joining any of the works of God, consistently look for opportunities to share the good news that the Messiah has come for all nations. Their involvement in all the diverse works of God provides amazing opportunities to share the good news of the Messiah. The Great Commission is given to all, but some are called to make that the focus of their lives. Sent-out ones are one part of the body of Christ that goes to peoples and places where the gospel is not and leaves New Testament churches. All believers join them in this task by praying, giving, and going as God provides opportunities. The gifts of all believers can help the missionary team if they are called to go for a season. However, sent-out ones must go where the gospel is not and leave New Testament churches. This is sent-out ones' place under the Son. This is how missionaries fit into the mission of God.

ENDNOTES

[1] Special thanks to David Wiggins and Jacob Boss for the invitation.

[2] F. F. Bruce, *The Book of the Acts, Revised Edition* (New International Commentary on the New Testament; Grand Rapids: William B. Eerdmans Publishing Company, 1988), 3.

[3] This will be the focus of chapter one.

[4] This will be the focus of chapter two.

[55] This will be the focus of chapter three.

[6] This will be the focus of chapter four.

[7] John Polhill, *Acts* (New American Commentary; Nashville, TN: Broadman Press, 1992), 79-80.

[8] Gabriel's appearance to Zechariah powerfully identified John the Baptist as the forerunner who prepares the way for none other than the LORD (Mal 3:1) and Jesus as the one promised to reign on David's throne forever (Luke 1:26-33).

[9] In Luke one, God the Father is clearly identified as Savior and Lord (Luke 1:16, 32, 47) and then in Luke two the angel announces that the child who has been born is the "Savior, who is Christ the Lord" (Luke 2:11).

[10] The ESV Study Bible outlines this section of Luke as "The Ministry of Jesus in Galilee (Luke 4:16-9:50)."

[11] NASB, ESV have "that" translating the word *hina* (ἵνα) which here introduces a purpose clause.

[12] Here Luke reflects John's approach writing decades later. John recorded many fewer miracles and called them signs. The purpose of the miracles was often to make Jesus' identity certain, like Luke is doing in these chapters.

[13] The *ESV Study Bible* (Wheaton, Ill.: Crossway Bibles, 2008) outlines this section, "Jesus, Lord of nature, demons, disease, and death (Luke 8:22-56)."

[14] From the perspective that his resurrection was not so much what Jesus did, but "God the Father who raised him from the dead" (Gal 1:1). John records the second miraculous catch of fish at the Sea of Tiberias, following the resurrection (John 21:4-11).

[15] Author's translation of Luke 24:19 emphasizing the use of *ergō* (ἔργῳ) in this verse, on resurrection day. The connection of the word to the topic at hand will be described later in this chapter and the next. This translation follows the ESV's translation in 2 Thess 2:17, the only other place the exact Greek phrase "work and word" (*ergō kai lógō,* ἔργῳ καὶ λόγῳ) is found in the New Testament, which also points out to the English reader the normal translation of *ergon* (ἔργον) as work or works.

[16] The concluding verses of Luke are so central to our discussion that they are the topic of an entire chapter, chapter three below.

[17] F. F. Bruce takes this position, "This exactly summarizes the scope of the Gospel of Luke from 4:1 onward... The implication of Luke's words is that his second volume will be an account of what Jesus *continued* to do and teach after his ascension—no longer in visible presence on earth but by his Spirit in his followers. The expression "to do and teach" well sums up the twofold subject matter of all the canonical Gospels" they all record *The Work and Words of Jesus*" (*Acts*, 30.)

[18] The word choice of NASB "works" is also found in KJV and NKJV. ESV uses the synonym "deeds."

[19] The very common words "the works," τὰ ἔργα, *ta erga,* is used in Matt 11:2 and in the Greek translation, the LXX, of Psa 111:2.

[20] The Greek translation of the Old Testament uses *ta erga* (τὰ ἔργα) for "work."

[21] Emphasis added. The Greek translation of the Old Testament uses *ta erga* (τὰ ἔργα) for "works."

[22] Dr. Morris had a great perspective on the way water and rainfall were described in Scripture as his Ph.D. was in hydraulic engineering from the University of Minnesota. (Henry Morris, *The Remarkable Record of Job* (Green Forest, AR, Master Books, 2000), p. 37.)

[23] The NIV translates the Hebrew "care for" which is consistent with the idea of visiting to oversee, one meaning of "פָּקַד *pâqad*; a primitive root meaning to visit (with friendly or hostile intent); by analogy, to oversee, muster, charge, *care for*, miss, deposit," (Olive Tree Enhanced Strong's Dictionary for ESV, referenced in Olive Tree software, emphasis added).

[24] Friburg's *Analytical Greek Lexicon* and Thayer's *Greek-English Lexicon of the New Testament* both specifically list creation as the translation of κτίσις *ktisis* in Rom 1:25. The NET uses "creation," NIV "created things," CSB "something created." From BibleWorks X software.

[25] The Greek translation of the Old Testament uses *ta erga* (τὰ ἔργα) for "the work."

[26] David J. Bosch, *Transforming Mission: Paradigm Shifts in Theology of Mission* (Maryknoll, NY: Orbis Books, 1991), 391. See pages 389-393 for a description of the historical development of the use of the term.

[27] Christopher Wright, in *The Mission of God: Unlocking the Bible's Grand Narrative* (Downers Grove, IL: IVP Academic, 2006), says "*Missional* is simply an adjective denoting something that is related to or characterized by mission, or has the qualities, attributes or dynamics of mission" (24).

[28] Christopher Wright says Jesus "was setting their hermeneutical orientation and agenda" (*ibid.*, 30) or "the central hermeneutical key... the hermeneutical matrix for our reading of the whole Bible" (*ibid.*, 31).

[29] Norval Geldenhuys, *The Gospel of Luke*, (The New International Commentary on the New Testament 4; Grand Rapids: Eerdmans, 1979), 634. Emphasis added.

[30] Tom Elliff, *What Should I Say to My Friend*, edited by Kim P. Davis, (Richmond, VA: International Mission Board, 2009), 53.

[31] Luke 24:44 begins with "Then" suggesting a continuation of the setting of the previous verse. (Darrell L. Bock in *Luke* (NIV Application Commentary Series; Grand Rapids: Zondervan, 1996, electronic edition referenced in Olive Tree Software) says, "Jesus now explains what has taken place," tying this paragraph to the setting of the previous setting. Eckhard J. Schnabel takes this view in *Acts* (Exegetical Commentary on the New Testament; Grand Rapids: Zondervan, 2012), 126. In contrast, Geldenhuys takes the closing two paragraphs to have taken place later during the forty days, (*Luke*, 641).)

[32] In *The Mission of God*, Christopher Wright masterfully shows that all the diverse works of God found in Scripture can be included in Jesus' outline in Luke 24:46-47. The forgiveness of sins that follows repentance will, in a sense, bring to culmination all the mission of God. In this present work, we are taking the wording of Luke 24:47 more narrowly. Since the gospel of Luke provides an exposition of Luke 24:46, the book of Acts provides Luke's explanation of 24:47. The second half of Jesus' overview states specifically that "repentance... should be proclaimed," the proclamation that forgiveness of sins based on repentance and faith in the Messiah's work should be proclaimed to all nations. Taken at their face value, these words seem much more narrow than all the works of God. In the book of Acts this proclamation of repentance to all nations happened (and continues to happen) as ordinary believers share the gospel wherever they are scattered in life (think of the unnamed believers of Acts 11) and as sent-out ones take the gospel where it is not (Acts 13-28). In both examples in Acts, the spread of the gospel naturally leads to church planting. This, as we will show, is the heart of the missionary task.

[33] Christopher Wright says, "The ultimate redemptive purpose of God lay elsewhere, invested in the tenuous human vessel of the ageing husband of a barren wife" (*Mission of God,* 202).

[34] We are dividing the Old Testament into three sections: Creation to Abraham, Abraham to David and David to the Prophets. This follows the overview of Matt 1:1 which points to Jesus Christ as descendant of Abraham and David.

[35] For an excellent discussion of the connection of Exod 20:10 and Heb 12:25 see Walter C. Kaiser, Jr.'s, article, "Israel's Missionary Call" in *Perspectives on the World Christian Movement: A Reader* (Pasadena, CA: William Carey Library, 1999), 13.

[36] "Work" translates *erga* (ἔργα).

[37] F. F. Bruce, *The Epistle to the Hebrews* (The New International Commentary on the New Testament; Grand Rapids, MI: Wm. B. Eerdmans Publishing Co, 1964), 21.

[38] Emphasis added. David L. Allen, *Hebrews* (The New American Commentary 35; Nashville, TN: B&H Publishing, 2010), 183-184.

[39] Rick Warren, "God Designed You for More," April 3, 2021, online at https://pastorrick.com/god-designed-you-for-ore/?utm_source=ActiveCampaignamp&vgo_e   e=fzrzbNdiQZrWKkgbsq-49TUzkASpiHornD%2Fz2wZTd1jg%3D. Cited on 4 April 2021.

[40] F. F. Bruce wrote, "These words of 1 Cor. 12:13 sum up the other aspect of Paul's distinctive doctrine of the Spirit. Baptism in the Spirit (the baptizer being Christ himself) is not simply an individual experience; it is the divine act by which believers in Christ are incorporated into his body" (F. F. Bruce, *The Epistles to the Colossians, to Philemon, and to the Ephesians* (The New International Commentary on the New Testament; Grand Rapids, MI: Wm. B. Eerdmans Publishing Co,, 1984), 234).

[41] The International Mission Board defines a missionary like this, "An IMB missionary is a disciple of Jesus set apart by the Holy Spirit, sent out from the church, and affirmed by the IMB to cross geographic, cultural, and/or linguistic barriers as part of a missionary team that is focused on making disciples and multiplying churches among unreached peoples and places." From https://www.imb.org/topic-term/imb-missionary-missionary-team/ cited on 20 Mar 2021.

[42] This will be the topic of chapter five.

[43] This will be the topic of chapter six.

[44] This will be the topic of chapter seven.

[45] What is clear is that Jesus had commanded the apostles to wait until the anointing of the Spirit. The naming of an apostle doesn't seem like waiting. The Old Testament passages, quoted in Acts one, do not specify when a replacement for Judas should be named nor that the eleven were authorized to replace him. The Old Testament passages simply make clear he was to be replaced. Finally, in church history, this passage has been harmfully used to suggest that men have been named to continue in Peter's seat with the authority of the original apostles. G. Campbell Morgan suggested that the naming of Matthias was not correct, "And again—this is a debated point in interpretation—but my own conviction is that we have a revelation of their inefficiency for organization; that the election of Matthias was wrong... He was a good man, but the wrong man for this position, and he passed out of sight; and when presently we come to the final glory of the city of God, we see twelve foundation stones, and twelve apostles' names, and I am not prepared to omit Paul from the twelve, believing that he was God's man for the filling of the gap." *The Acts of the Apostles* (New York: Fleming H. Revell, 1924), 21.

[46] The word encouragement is based on the verb *parakaleō* (παρακαλέω) to call to one's side, or to call alongside.

[47] David Hesselgrave, *Planting Churches Cross-Culturally: North America and Beyond* (2d. ed.; Grand Rapids: Baker, 2000), 96.

[48] Craig Bloomberg, *1 Corinthians* (The NIV Application Commentary 7; Grand Rapids, MI: Zondervan, 1994), 247.

[49] Don Dent, *The Ongoing Role of Apostles in Missions; The Forgotten Foundation* (Bloomington, IN, WestBow Press, 2019), xvii.

[50] F.F. Bruce, *Paul: Apostle of the Heart Set Free* (Grand Rapids: Eerdmans, 1977), 314–315.

[51] Eckhard J. Schnabel, *Paul the Missionary: Realities, Strategies and Methods* (Downers Grove, Ill.: IVP Academic, 2008), 132.

[52] "Apostles Even Now," in *Discovering the Mission of God: Best Missional Practices for the 21st Century* (ed. Mike Barnett and Robin Martin; Downers Grove, Ill.: IVP Academic, 2012), 355–69.

[53] Mark 16:14-18 would also apply to this setting.

[54] **Resurrection Appearances**
    1 – Mary, John 20:14
    2 – Women, Matt 28:9
    3 – Peter, Luke 24:34; **1 Cor 15:5**

4 – Two on the road from Jerusalem to Emmaus, Luke 24:15; Mark 16:12

5 – The Eleven (10) in the Jerusalem room, John 20:19; Luke 24:36; **1 Cor 15:5**

6 – The Eleven including Thomas in the Jerusalem room, John 20:6; Mark 16:14; (**1 Cor 15:5**)

7 – Peter and six disciples at the Sea, John 21:4

8 – The Commission on a Galilean mountain, Matt 28:16; **1 Cor 15:6**

9 – James, **1 Cor 15:7**

10 – The Ascension near Jerusalem, Acts 1:6-9; **1 Cor 15:7b**

[55] Leon Morris, *The First Epistle of Paul to the Corinthians* (Tyndale New Testament Commentaries; Cambridge, U.K.: William B. Eerdmans Publishing Company, 1981), 206.

[56] A. T. Robertson, *Word Pictures in the New Testament,* vol. 4 (Nashville: Broadman Press, 1930), 188.

[57] Thomas had been so extremely skeptical that he had responded to the testimony of the others, "Unless I see in his hands the mark of the nails, and place my finger into the mark of the nails, and place my hand into his side, I will never believe" (John 20:25). Praise God for a witness who wanted to be certain!

[58] A. T. Robertson explained, "The reference is not to the eleven who were all now convinced after some doubt, but to the others present. Paul states that over five hundred were present, most of whom were still alive when he wrote (1 Cor 15:6). It is natural that some should hesitate to believe so great a thing at the first appearance of Jesus to them. Their very doubt makes it easier for us to believe. This was the mountain where Jesus had promised to meet them. This fact explains the large number present. Time and place were arranged beforehand. It was the climax of the various appearances and in Galilee where were so many believers" (*Word Pictures,* v. 1, 244).

[59] F. F. Bruce describes Acts 2 as the "first Christian church" in *Acts*, 72. Millard J. Erickson, in *Christian Theology* (Grand Rapids, MI, 1985), concludes "the church originated at Pentecost" (p. 1048). John Hammett, in *Biblical Foundations for Baptist Churches: A Contemporary Ecclesiology*, (Grand Rapids, MI: Kregel Publications, 2005), writes, "The implication is that the church was not given birth until after Christ's earthly ministry" (p. 28).

Of course, if one is referring to the universal church consisting of all the redeemed of all the ages then you could say the Great Commission was given to the church universal, or all believers.

[60] The exact word and form, *poreuthéntes* (πορευθέντες), is used 15 times in the NT. Nine times it is followed by an imperative and every one of those nine is translated as an imperative in the English: "Go" (Matt 2:8; 9:13; 11:4; 28:19; Mk 16:15; Luke 7:22; 13:32; 17:14; 22:8). Six times it is not followed by an imperative and is not translated in English as a command (Matt 21:6; 22:15; 27:66; Luke 9:12, 13, 62). This would underline the normal assumption to translate with an imperative.

[61] Herschel Hobbs, *The Gospel of Matthew* (Proclaiming the New Testament; Nashville: Broadman Press, 1961), 132.

[62] Rick Warren, *The Purpose-Driven Church* (Grand Rapids, MI: Zondervan, 1995), 104. Italics in original.

[63] Craig Blomberg, *Matthew* (The New American Commentary 22; Nashville, TN: B&H Publishing, 1992), 431.

[64] While the noun deacon is not found in Acts six, the verb to "deac" or to serve is used, hence, they were likely the first deacons.

[65] The rapture word is used in the Greek (*harpazō*, ἁρπάζω). Since the next verse says Philip "found himself" at Azotus, it is not really clear how he got there. I like to say, Short term missionary service can be an amazing trip.

[66] To borrow Paul's language that he used decades later.

[67] "The expressions 'not from [*apo*] men nor by [*dia*] man' indicate that Paul's apostolic vocation neither originated nor was mediated by human agency" (Timothy George, *Galatians* (The New American Commentary v.30, Nashville: Broadman & Holman Publishers, 1994), 80).

[68] This will be the focus of the next chapter.

[69] Bosch, *Transforming Mission*, 91.

[70] It could cause one to wonder if the others are really commissions if they don't have a command. The Mark 16:15 passage is not found in the oldest Greek manuscripts, as noted in many English translations.

[71] Baptism by the Spirit puts the believer into the body of Christ, the church universal (1 Cor 12:13), whereas water baptism appears to be the means to unite with a local congregation (Acts 2:47).

[72] The idea of multiplication goes back to God's first recorded words to human beings in Gen 1:28, repeated to Noah (Gen 9:1, 7), Abraham (Gen 22:17), Isaac

(Gen 26:4), Jacob (Gen 35:11; 48:4) and the entire nation (Lev 26:9; Deut 7:13; Isa 51:2; Jer 33:22). In the New Testament Jesus switched from physical multiplication to spiritual (Matt 13:3, 8-9: Luke 8:11; Matt 13:37-38), a change continued in Acts (Acts 6:7; 8:1, 4; 9:31; 11:19).

[73] "And he said, 'Then I beg you, father, to send him to my father's house—for I have five brothers—so that he may warn them, lest they also come into this place of torment'" (Luke 16:27-28).

[74] Don't miss the use of "the work" to describe what missionaries were sent to do. God's works include the missionary task!

[75] Some call Lydia a person of peace, but there is no clear textual basis. Acts 18 provides an undeniable example.

[76] Paul looks back to these early days in the epistle he sent years later and speaks of their support (Phil 4:15-16).

[77] The detail the New Testament emphasizes about the synagogues is that the Scriptures were read there each week, as seen in Acts 15:21; 13:15, 27 and Luke 4:16-17. Remember, "Faith comes from hearing, and hearing through the word of Christ" (Rom 10:17). David Garrison has noted the value of having as many people as possible reading Scripture as a great form of Abundant Gospel Sowing in *Church Planting Movements Movements: How God Is Redeeming a Lost World* (WIGTake Resources, 2004).

[78] 1 Thessalonians was written as little as three months after Paul's departure and he was able to say to them, "And you became imitators of us and of the Lord, for you received the word in much affliction, with the joy of the Holy Spirit, so that you became *an example to all the believers* in Macedonia and in Achaia" (1 Thess 1:6-7, emphasis added).

[79] After Corinth they went to Ephesus (Acts 18:24-27), then returned to Rome (Rom 16:5) before going back to Ephesus (2 Tim 4:19).

[80] Acts 11:27-30; Acts 18:5; Phil 4:16; 1 Cor 16:1-2; 2 Cor 11:9. This seems consistent with Matt 10:9; Mark 6:8; Luke 9:3; 10:4; John 6:27.

[81] Elbert Smith. *Church Planting by the Book* (Fort Washington, PA: CLC Publications, 2015), Kindle Edition, location 802 of 2617.

[82] Both phrases use forms of the word "many" (*polús*, πολύς).

[83] While we may love to know more about Paul's previous ministry in Arabia (Gal 1:17-18) or Tarsus (Acts 9:30), the New Testament has not specifically described a longer period of ministry in one city up to this point.

[84] Nothing in the text suggests they were already Christians.

Made in the USA
Columbia, SC
15 August 2022